"Scrupulous in its fairness to Judais[m] ... cor-
recting noxious Christian misrep[resentations] ...
and engaging little book succeeds [in presenting the]
Christian apostle to the gentiles, wit[h ...]
formed and which he never thought h[e had left. Both Chris-]
tians and Jews have much to gain from reading *A Jewish Paul*. Highly
recommended!"

—Jon D. Levenson, Harvard University

"Since the middle of the twentieth century, debates have raged in aca-
demia over the question of Paul's relationship to Judaism. Yet these
debates remain scarcely known to the public. Matthew Thiessen seeks
to remedy that situation in this book, and he succeeds admirably in
clear and cogent prose. But the book is not *merely* an introduction to debates over Paul and Judaism; Thiessen does not plod neutrally through
various scholarly positions. He makes a strong case that Paul remained
fully and firmly within Judaism from birth to death. Thiessen is not
the first to make this argument, but he does it with a notable twist:
he argues that the best framework for understanding the historical
Paul lies in the portrait bequeathed to us by the author of Luke-Acts.
It is a compelling argument, sure to hold the attention of seasoned
scholars while providing uninitiated readers a clear introduction to
this important debate."

—Pamela Eisenbaum, Iliff School of Theology

"Ever since E. P. Sanders's pioneering work, the role of Judaism has
been an important dimension of work on Paul's letters. In this very
readable volume, Thiessen provides the reader with a portrait of Paul
that takes his Jewishness with the seriousness it deserves. The debate
on many issues he engages will not be brought to closure, but he charts
directions that all scholars will need to consider going forward."

—Gary A. Anderson, University of Notre Dame

"God bless Matthew Thiessen! It is so difficult to give a historically
compelling account of the apostle Paul that is, at the same time, helpful
to readers of Christian Scripture and, on top of all that, readable and
accessible. I know because I have tried. Now, though, I will be very
happy simply to refer people to this wonderful book."

—Matthew V. Novenson, University of Edinburgh

"This is an excellent introduction to Paul. It is concise, clear, and nuanced. It will be a real feast to scholars, students, and interested readers. The book can be used in various contexts (seminaries, religious studies programs, or church Bible studies). I cannot recommend Thiessen's *A Jewish Paul* enough for serious and important conversations between Jews and Christians."

—**Ronald Charles**, University of Toronto

"In *A Jewish Paul*, Matthew Thiessen offers an introduction to Paul that is genuinely fresh, thoroughly stimulating, and highly accessible. Drawing on some of his signature contributions to Pauline studies as well as new material, Thiessen offers provocative readings that challenge long-standing interpretations that fail to recognize Paul's identity as a first-century Jewish thinker. All who consider themselves students of Paul—whether the beginner or the scholar—will find themselves engrossed in this book's pages."

—**Michael Patrick Barber**, Augustine Institute Graduate School of Theology

"The apostle Paul may need no introduction. Few people—perhaps only Jesus himself—are as widely known as the man from Tarsus. In fact, Paul may be *too* well known, and his robust reputation may prevent us from seeing him with historical or theological clarity. Matthew Thiessen offers students and scholars alike an invaluable resource: an accessible-yet-innovative introduction to a *Jewish* Paul, the herald of Israel's Messiah to the non-Jewish nations."

—**Rafael Rodríguez**, Johnson University

"Excellent scholars who work at the cutting edge of their field and who have a mastery of its history (as does Thiessen on Pauline studies) are sometimes unable to communicate that field to those outside of it. This book is an outstanding exception. It is as readable as it is masterful. This is fortunate, because its message could not possibly be more important if Christians and New Testament scholars alike are to finally escape the gross misreadings of Paul that continuously put Jewish lives in danger of violence."

—**Sara Parks**, St. Francis Xavier University

A
Jewish
Paul

A Jewish Paul

The *Messiah's Herald* to the *Gentiles*

Matthew Thiessen

Baker Academic
a division of Baker Publishing Group
Grand Rapids, Michigan

© 2023 by Matthew Thiessen

Published by Baker Academic
a division of Baker Publishing Group
PO Box 6287, Grand Rapids, MI 49516-6287
www.bakeracademic.com

Printed in the United States of America

Library of Congress Cataloging-in-Publication Data
Names: Thiessen, Matthew, 1977– author.
Title: A Jewish Paul : the Messiah's herald to the gentiles / Matthew Thiessen.
Description: Grand Rapids, Michigan : Baker Academic, a division of Baker
    Publishing Group, [2023] | Includes bibliographical references and index.
Identifiers: LCCN 2022057954 | ISBN 9781540965714 (paperback) | ISBN
    9781540966629 (casebound) | ISBN 9781493441761 (ebook) | ISBN
    9781493441778 (pdf)
Subjects: LCSH: Bible. Epistles of Paul—Theology. | Judaism—History—Post-
    exilic period, 586 B.C.–210 A.D. | Christianity and other religions—Judaism. |
    Judaism—Relations—Christianity.
Classification: LCC BS2651 .T45 2023 | DDC 227/.06—dc23/eng/20230303
LC record available at https://lccn.loc.gov/2022057954

Baker Publishing Group publications use paper produced from sustainable forestry practices and post-consumer waste whenever possible.

23   24   25   26   27   28   29   7   6   5   4   3   2   1

For Solomon and Maggie

Contents

Acknowledgments

In the winter of 2020, I was eagerly looking forward to early April because it meant the end of the academic term. Stretched out ahead of me lay not only a long spring and summer of research, hiking, and camping but also a fall research leave to begin a new writing project. Those plans were not to be.

A worldwide pandemic broke out, my university went online, libraries closed, and our kids were required to continue their educations from home. Ultimately, these were but minor inconveniences when compared to the millions who have died from Covid-19 (and who continue to do so), to the many who have lost loved ones, to those suffering from long-term effects from Covid-19, and to those who have faced financial loss or even ruin. But minor as they were, these inconveniences quickly led me to realize that my research and writing goals would need to change.

Instead of breaking into a new area of research, I decided to write an introduction to Paul that showed how he could be read intelligibly but without the common anti-Jewish baggage that attends most interpretations of his letters. This short book, then, is my effort to familiarize a wide range of people to one way of reading Paul that is growing in popularity due to an effort to depict a more historically plausible reading of Paul and one that might just be more theologically fruitful, especially with regard to the relationship between Judaism and Christianity, Jews and Christians.

I want to express my gratitude to the entire Baker Academic staff but especially to my editor, Bryan Dyer, and associate editors, Jennifer Koenes and Melisa Blok, who have helped bring this book to life. Most of this book was written in fits and starts as my spouse and I struggled to juggle the at-home and online education of our two children, her cooking business, and my teaching and research. This book is dedicated to my children, Solomon and Maggie, reluctant hiking partners, curious minds, and relentless troublemakers. I love you both with every cell of my body!

Introduction

The earliest surviving statement about Paul's letters describes them in the following way: "There are some things in them hard to understand, which the ignorant and unstable twist to their own destruction" (2 Pet. 3:16 NRSVue). That might be a disturbing acknowledgment, especially for those who read Paul's writings as sacred scripture. If someone much closer to Paul's day, someone who shared many of Paul's cultural assumptions, considered Paul difficult to comprehend, then how likely is it that we modern readers will understand him? It's a potentially troubling claim for another reason too: it contradicts what some Christians call the "doctrine of the perspicuity" (or in regular English, the "clarity") of the Bible. Consider, for instance, the words of Martin Luther, one of the key figures of the Protestant Reformation, on the Bible's clear message: "It is true that for many people much remains abstruse; but this is not due to the obscurity of Scripture but to the blindness or indolence of those who will not take the trouble to look at the very clearest truth."[1]

Luther here places the blame for any difficulties readers might have in interpreting the Bible on the readers themselves. It's their fault, one arising out of human blasphemy and perversity, not the Bible's fault. But contrary to Luther, the author of 2 Peter states (perspicuously, I might add) that it is Paul's letters themselves that are, at least in places, obscure and therefore challenging to interpret. And it is their

---

1. Luther, *Bondage of the Will*, 166.

very obscurity that makes them susceptible to misuse and to being twisted. It is 2 Peter's assessment of Paul's letters that later came to be preserved within the boundaries of the New Testament and consequently stands as a canonical judgment *for Christians* on just how obscure parts of Paul's letters are. To admit, then, that Paul's letters are difficult to understand, and therefore to be willing to question whether common readings of his letters are accurate, is not only fair game but also downright biblical. Beware of any person who claims that Paul's letters are crystal clear or who asserts that they understand everything in them.

The state of the academic study of Paul almost two thousand years after Paul wrote proves just how accurate this early evaluation of his thinking was. Readers of Paul's letters live around the globe and in the twenty-first century, not in the first-century Mediterranean world. His world, his culture(s), his language are not ours. The assumptions and knowledge that he shared with many of his first readers and hearers are not necessarily our own. Like paleontologists, we can dig into Paul's context through other ancient texts or through archaeological remains,[2] but much of his world and much of his thinking will forever be lost or obscure to us.

Likewise, *our* assumptions, *our* cultures, and *our* knowledge were not Paul's. The expectations you and I as modern people bring to our readings of Paul without even knowing it would probably surprise us. It is as impossible for us to shed these expectations when reading Paul as it is to be aware of them all. We know how the last two thousand years have turned out, and we read and write and live in light of that knowledge. We know that the small groups that Paul organized and to whom he wrote letters grew into something we now call *the church* and *Christianity*. And we know that the church and Christianity are distinct from another religion: Judaism.[3] We know that Christianity soon debated things like the precise relationship between Jesus and

---

2. For instance, see the impressive work of Nasrallah, *Archaeology and the Letters of Paul*.

3. This statement oversimplifies things, as it ignores messianic Jews, who see no contradiction in following and worshiping Jesus and living as law-observant Jews.

Israel's God and the contents of what would come to be called the New Testament (and the Old Testament). Paul knew none of this, since he, to quote Paula Fredriksen, "lived his life—as we all must live our lives—innocent of the future."[4] Given the fact that some of Paul's earliest readers found his letters difficult to interpret, what are modern readers to do, since we neither share many of Paul's assumptions nor have full access to the broadly shared "encyclopedia" of information available to both Paul and his first readers? Should we give up Paul's letters as ancient relics whose meaning is now lost to us? Or is there a way to help make sense of them?

Most people, perhaps even a good percentage of Christian clergy, likely remain unaware of the fact that people who spend their careers studying and writing on Paul disagree quite strongly with each other about what he says.[5] Even those of us who have dedicated parts or all of our careers to thinking and writing about Paul struggle to make sense of Paul's different letters, to take occasional writings and provide a coherent, if inevitably incomplete, account of what he thought. In recent decades we have seen longer and longer books outlining Paul's thinking. To get a sense of this exegetical (and theological) arms race, where longer seems to be equated with better, take these three examples: in 1997 James Dunn published *The Theology of Paul the Apostle* (844 pages), in 2009 Douglas Campbell published *The Deliverance of God* (1,248 pages), and in 2013 N. T. Wright published *Paul and the Faithfulness of God* (1,700 pages). I don't believe there exists a longer treatment of Paul's theology, but given this trend, the next big book on Paul should be at least 2,100 pages in length.

This little book does not seek to be exhaustive. I won't discuss every verse or even every theme in Paul's letters. Instead, I seek to introduce readers to one particularly thorny question: How does Paul relate to the Judaism (or, perhaps better, Judaism*s*) of his day? This is a historical question, but for modern Christians (and any interested Jews) it is a historical question that has theological and ecumenical relevance.

4. Fredriksen, *Paul*, xii.
5. For one recent attempt to bring some of these interpretations into conversation, see McKnight and Oropeza, *Perspectives on Paul.*

Does Paul condemn and abandon Judaism? Does he view it as something inferior or at least outdated in the wake of Jesus? If so, how should Christians today think about Judaism and relate to Jews? Looking back over the last two thousand years, we know that most Christians have viewed Judaism as inferior or even pernicious, something left behind or something that has died.[6] Consequently, many Christians have treated individual Jews and Jewish communities with contempt, revulsion, hatred, and violence. Paul's letters have frequently served as scriptural support for Christian anti-Judaism.

Is it possible that there is a different way to read Paul's letters, one that does not denigrate Judaism? The question of Paul's relationship to Judaism has dominated Pauline scholarship over the last several decades, resulting in (at least) four ways that academics have tried to make sense of Paul's writings as they relate to Judaism; these four ways are commonly called the "Lutheran," "new perspective," "apocalyptic," and "radical new perspective" (or "Paul within Judaism") readings. Some of these "schools" may be more familiar to readers than others. But remember, familiarity doesn't necessarily mean that such a reading is correct.

Most well known, and likely an interpretation of Paul's letters that many readers think is the only way one could possibly understand him, is what scholars frequently refer to as the Lutheran perspective on Paul. Outside of a few circles, people reading this book have probably not heard a sermon or been in a Sunday school where they heard someone claim they were preaching the *Lutheran* view of Paul, so I find this name unhelpful. Instead, I prefer to use the same sort of language that the "Lutheran" view uses in its attempt to summarize or make Paul's thinking coherent. For this reason, I call this dominant reading the anti-legalistic or anti-works-righteousness reading of Paul. Briefly put, this reading of Paul argues (or assumes) that ancient Judaism was a religion of works righteousness and legalism. Supposedly, Jews believed that they needed to do enough good deeds to merit God's saving acts, and so they focused their efforts on keeping the Jewish law.

6. Newman, "Death of Judaism."

According to this view, at one time Paul too held this conviction, but he came to the realization that all people had sinned. Or as he put it, "All have sinned and lack the glory of God" (Rom. 3:23). Consequently, he concluded that no person could possibly earn God's deliverance. Again, in Paul's own words, "Now it is evident that no one is justified before God by the law" (Gal. 3:11); "all flesh will not be justified by the works of the law" (Gal. 2:16); "for 'all flesh will not be justified in his sight' by works of the law" (Rom. 3:20). Here Paul quotes from Psalm 143:2 (Septuagint [hereafter LXX] 142:2), which states, "Do not enter into judgment with your slave, because every living being [Greek: *pas zōn*] will not be justified before you." Paul's assessment, then, of the human predicament was exceedingly bleak.

But he found the solution to the sinful human condition in the realization that God would save people apart from human works and through faith in Jesus: "We know that a person is justified not by the works of the law but through the faithfulness of Jesus the Messiah" (Gal. 2:16); "we consider that a person is justified by faith(fulness) apart from works of the law" (Rom. 3:28). What humans could not do to earn God's blessing and gifts, God accomplished in the Messiah.[7] The anti-legalistic reading of Paul, then, regularly assumes that Jews believed one needed to and could earn one's deliverance through good deeds. Paul condemned this purportedly Jewish view as legalistic and as a form of works righteousness, both of which were odious to God. In contrast to this Jewish legalism, Paul advocated that one needed only to believe that Jesus saved people through his atoning death on the cross.

But in 1977 E. P. Sanders argued that there was a fundamental problem with this common understanding of Paul: it depended on an account of ancient Judaism that was both historically inaccurate and theologically dismissive. Many Jewish texts demonstrate that at least some Jews did not think people could simply earn God's saving action or that anyone could live a sinless life.[8] For instance, the Chronicler states, "There is no one who does not sin" (2 Chron. 6:36

---

7. To my mind, the most careful argument for this general position is Westerholm, *Perspectives Old and New on Paul.*
8. Sanders, *Paul and Palestinian Judaism.*

NRSVue). Qohelet (or Ecclesiastes) makes a similarly dreary claim: "Surely there is no one on earth so righteous as to do good without ever sinning" (7:20 NRSVue). And in the second century BCE, the author of the Book of Luminaries avers that "no one of the flesh can be just before the Lord" (1 Enoch 81.5). This latter statement is remarkably similar to Paul's repeated claim that no *flesh* will be justified before God (Rom. 3:20; Gal. 2:16). Such examples could fill pages, but these three pithy statements prove that at least some Jews believed *all* humans were guilty of sinning.[9] Other Jews, such as the author of the Prayer of Manasseh, believed that there were a righteous few but that most people were sinners and desperately needed God's unmerited grace and mercy:

> O Lord, according to your great goodness
> you have promised repentance and forgiveness
> to those who have sinned against you,
> and in the multitude of your mercies
> you have appointed repentance for sinners,
> so that they may be saved. (Prayer of Manasseh 7 NRSVue)

For this and other reasons, Sanders argued that early Judaism was neither legalistic nor a religion of works righteousness but could be described as a system of covenantal nomism. That is, Jews believed God had graciously chosen Israel prior to and apart from any good works they had done. Israel's covenantal response to God's election was to respond with faithful and grateful law observance. For Sanders, Judaism stressed that keeping the Jewish law was the right response to God's prior and gracious election of Israel. But even this response to God's grace was not expected to be perfect. The entire wilderness tent complex (and later temples) and its rituals and sacrifices, which were at the heart of life for many Jews, imply that errors and sins would occur regularly. For this reason, God gave Israel the merciful means to deal with any such sins through the cultic prac-

---

9. For a rich account of the varieties of ancient Jewish thinking on sin and evil, see Brand, *Evil Within and Without*.

tices related to the wilderness tent and temple, especially the Day of Atonement.

But if Sanders is correct, what should we make of Paul's negative statements about works of the law? What was Paul fighting, if it wasn't legalism and vain attempts to curry God's favor? Several interpreters, most prominently James D. G. Dunn and N. T. Wright, have suggested that Paul's problem with Judaism was that it was ethnocentric, a reading that they call a "new perspective" on Paul.[10] In this reading, Paul's attack on works of the law was an attack not on doing generic good deeds but on Jewish reliance on the *Jewish* law. For both scholars, the phrase *works of the law* refers especially to aspects of the Jewish law that mark one off as Jewish: things like the rite of circumcision, Sabbath observance, and Jewish dietary regulations. According to Dunn and Wright, Jews misused the law both as a basis for ethnic pride and as a means to exclude gentiles from God's saving actions. Both have argued that Jewish ethnocentrism insisted that gentiles could be saved only through conversion to Judaism, in which gentiles took up, among other things, distinctively Jewish practices. For Paul, this problem became particularly acute because Jewish followers of Jesus insisted that non-Jewish followers of Jesus needed to undergo circumcision and adopt the law of Moses (see Acts 15:1, 5).

It is this purported misplaced pride in one's own cultural practices and insistence that other ethnic groups needed to adopt them to be pleasing to God that Paul condemns, not works righteousness. Not *works* versus grace, as in the anti-legalistic paradigm, but *race* versus grace. This reading approaches Paul's letters through an anti-ethnocentric lens: Paul's opponents thought God was the God of the Jews alone, but Paul had come to know better: God was the God not just of the Jews but also of the gentiles (Rom. 3:29).

Another school of interpretation often goes by the name of the "apocalyptic" reading of Paul. While this school draws on the groundbreaking work of Albert Schweitzer,[11] the proponents of this reading are

10. Dunn, *New Perspective on Paul*; Wright, *Paul and the Faithfulness of God*.
11. Schweitzer, *Mysticism of Paul the Apostle*.

more heavily indebted to Ernst Käsemann and J. Louis Martyn.[12] This school of interpretation stresses that when Israel's God revealed Jesus to Paul, Paul experienced a radical break from his past, including his Jewishness. Consequently, they point to Paul's statement in Galatians where he mentions his former way or conduct in something he calls *ioudaismos* (often translated as "Judaism"), as well as to Paul's claims that "if anyone is in the Messiah, there is a new creation: everything old has passed away; see, everything has become new" (2 Cor. 5:17; cf. Gal. 6:15). The apocalyptic reading of Paul stresses the newness of Paul's message and its radical discontinuity from Judaism: the Messiah's coming dissolves old structures of male and female, Jew and gentile, slave and free (Gal. 3:28).

Numerous elements within these readings are essential to the account I will give of Paul in the following pages. With the anti-legalistic reading, for instance, I believe that Paul does not think that people can earn God's favor. God's gift of deliverance to humanity is of such incomparable worth that no one can merit it. But I don't think that Paul disagreed here with his fellow Jews, since they too believed in God's deliverance as a divinely offered and humanly unmerited gift.[13] And in agreement with the anti-ethnocentric reading, I believe that one must read Paul's letters in relation to ethnic distinctions, albeit ethnicity as defined by ancient Jews, who divided the world between Jews and non-Jews—a group that they often lumped together under the generic title "the nations," which I will translate as "gentiles."[14] But I don't think Paul's problem with Judaism was that it was ethnocentric. After all, Paul's own writings are just as ethnocentric as any

12. Käsemann, "Beginnings of Christian Theology," and Martyn, *Theological Issues in the Letters of Paul.*
13. In general see Barclay, *Paul and the Gift,* which shows the diversity of Jewish thinking about grace. In contrast to Barclay, though, I am convinced that most (perhaps all) Jews believed that one could not fully merit God's favor or gifts.
14. When you see the word *gentiles,* think not just in the generic sense—non-Jews—but also, as I will show later, of people who almost always worship the wrong gods and live immoral lives from a Jewish perspective. Additionally, Lopez, *Apostle to the Conquered,* makes a strong case that we should *also* think of gentiles as the defeated and subordinated Other in relation to the Roman Empire. And on the importance of placing Paul's thinking and actions in a diasporic setting, see Charles, *Paul and the Politics of Diaspora.*

other ancient Jewish writing, and much more so than many.[15] After all, Paul repeatedly says, "To the Jew first and then to the Greek" (Rom. 1:16; 2:9–10). And like the apocalyptic reading, I am convinced that Paul thought the Messiah's coming had ushered in the end of the ages and that Israel's God was indeed doing something new as the wake of the Messiah's resurrection rippled through the cosmos. But I don't think Paul's apocalypticism distinguished him from his fellow Jews or implied in any way a break with Judaism. Instead, the Messiah's coming, death, and resurrection were, for Paul, its *telos*—its goal or culmination—not its destruction (Rom. 10:4).

While I agree with many aspects of the major interpretations of Paul's writings, I categorically reject one conclusion at which they frequently arrive: that Paul must have thought something was inherently flawed with, wrong about, or absent from Judaism. Almost always these readings conclude that Paul's problem with Judaism was that it taught that people needed to work to earn favor with or deliverance from God. Or Paul's problem was that Judaism was characterized by ethnic pride and pushed ethnic practices onto others in a way analogous to Christian European colonialism. Or Paul's problem was that Judaism was part of the old order of the cosmos that the Messiah's coming had now destroyed, and so holding on to Jewish practices was to be guilty of clinging to archaic and obsolete structures and actions.

In the following pages, I will sketch a brief account of Paul's thinking in a way that seeks to situate him *within* and not *against* the Jewish world that was part of the larger ancient Mediterranean world. While I present my own account, it is one that shares many (but not all) things in common with a fourth stream of Pauline scholarship that has gone by a few different names: the *Sonderweg* reading of Paul associated with Lloyd Gaston and John Gager, the *radical new perspective* associated with Stanley Stowers and Pamela Eisenbaum, and the *Paul within Judaism* reading associated with William Campbell, Kathy Ehrensperger, Paula Fredriksen, Mark Nanos, and Magnus Zetterholm.[16] I confess that I am

---

15. See Novenson, *Last Man*; Ophir and Rosen-Zvi, *Goy*, chapter 5.
16. Gaston, *Paul and the Torah*; Gager, *Reinventing Paul*; Stowers, *Rereading of Romans*; Eisenbaum, *Paul Was Not a Christian*; W. Campbell, *Unity and Diversity in Christ*;

not particularly fond of any of these names but lack a better moniker to give this unruly "school" of interpreters. I would most closely connect the account of Paul that I will lay out in the following pages not to any one modern scholar but to an ancient writer, the author of the Gospel of Luke and the Acts of the Apostles.

This approach to Paul acknowledges that ancient Jews held different views on almost everything. Paul was one ancient Jew living and thinking and acting within a diverse Jewish world that sought to be faithful to Israel's God and Israel's law. The Acts of the Apostles, I think, provides early evidence of just this approach to understanding Paul, both the man and the message.

———————
Ehrensperger, *Searching Paul*; Fredriksen, *Paul*; Nanos, *Reading Paul within Judaism*; and Zetterholm, *Approaches to Paul*.

1

Making Paul Weird Again

Paul lived almost two thousand years ago. He lived and moved and had his being in the ancient Mediterranean world, a world that shared assumptions and beliefs that frequently differed from the assumptions and beliefs many of his later readers have held. Were we to somehow magically transport Paul to our world and were we able to bridge the language gap, I imagine that we would frequently conclude that Paul is a rather odd duck. Bibles and books on Paul seek to do just this, translating his Greek into modern languages while trying to make intelligible the various statements that make up his letters. This is important work, but at times the effort to make Paul

---

This chapter title was clearly influenced by Matthew Novenson, who in 2018 used the phrase in relation to the work of Paula Fredriksen. See Novenson, *Paul, Then and Now*, 133. Novenson is indebted to C. M. Chin ("Marvelous Things Heard," 480), who advocates for doing "weird history": "I would like to suggest, though, that the empathetic project of history, especially premodern history, is better served by a kind of imaginative stubbornness, a determination to remember that people living in past worlds were not always very much like us, but that we should pay attention to them anyway. And this much harder project of empathy is what I think focusing on weirdness allows us to undertake."

intelligible results in remaking Paul in our own image. How can we avoid this danger and allow Paul to be Paul in all of his strangeness?

Words matter. Sometimes the most common words matter the most because they carry with them hidden assumptions that bear serious ideological or, in the case of a figure like Paul, theological weight. You may have already noticed some less-than-common words and expressions in the introduction to this book. And you may have been surprised by some common words that are missing. Let me say a few words about words—why I avoid some and use others—and then connect the *why* of these words to the *what* of my broader methodological approach to thinking and talking about Paul.

Some of my biggest writing regrets are the translation choices I have made when talking about ancient texts. These choices usually weren't even conscious decisions but were my unthinking following of conventions from which I was too lazy or too ignorant to break away. Here I repent of using those words. I won't use the word *Christian* at any point to refer to followers of Jesus in the first century CE. Why not? Because the word never appears in Paul's letters. Although Paul never uses *Christian* (or *Christianity*), it appears three times in what we now call the New Testament, twice in Acts (11:26; 26:28) and once in 1 Peter (4:16). In all instances, it seems to be an outsider term applied to Jesus followers by the powers of the Roman Empire. In 1 Peter we see the author calling readers to bear this title with pride, even if it was intended to demean and insult.[1]

One could account for the absence of the word *Christian* in Paul's writings in one of two ways. First, it is possible that Paul just did not know the term and therefore could not use it. Most scholars doubt that either Acts or 1 Peter dates to Paul's lifetime. Consequently, it might be anachronistic to use the terms *Christian* or *Christianity* in relation to either Paul or the kinds of groups Paul organized and then addressed through his letter writing. Second, and perhaps more tantalizing, it is possible that the term *Christian* predates Acts and 1 Peter by some decades and that Paul knew the title but consciously chose not to use it.

---

1. Kotrosits, *Lives of Objects*, 104–5.

Why would he do this? Did he dislike the term? If that's the case, then our use of it to describe both him and his earliest readers would be not only anachronistic but also non-Pauline and possibly even un-Pauline.

For Paul, the human world was divided into two major groups: Jews and non-Jews. And within these two categories there were those people who followed Jesus and those who did not.

Figure 1.1

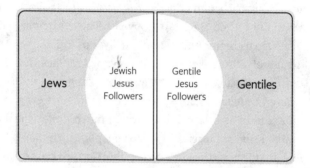

When *we* use the term *Christian*, we almost always assume that it is a category mutually exclusive of Judaism. Virtually all contemporary Christians and Jews hold that assumption, even as it (conveniently?) ignores the small number of messianic Jews who exist today.[2]

Figure 1.2

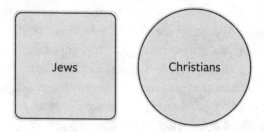

2. Even within this small community, there are significant distinctions. See the important work of Kinzer, *Postmissionary Messianic Judaism*, and Cohn-Sherbok, *Messianic Judaism*.

The term *Christian* brings with it a mental map of a world with a clearly defined and defended border between two distinct religions: Judaism and Christianity. To use the term of Paul's day would be just as inaccurate and unhelpful as calling the fourteenth-century Indigenous peoples of Turtle Island *Americans* or *Canadians* on the basis of whether they resided above or below what we now call the forty-ninth parallel. Canada and the United States did not exist in the fourteenth century, and the border we draw on maps is little more than a modern legal fiction (and, of course, parts of Canada are below the forty-ninth parallel, and parts of the United States are above it). These categories do not apply to or help us better understand the lives of Indigenous people.

Unfortunately, there is no simple one-word replacement for the word *Christian*. Most scholars who avoid this language resort to the use of *believers* or *followers*, and I will follow them here even as I find this language both awkward and anemic. I much prefer speaking of those loyal to Jesus or Messiah loyalists: people who not only believe something (that Jesus is the Messiah and that God has raised him from the dead) but also have committed their lives to and placed their hopes in this political figure.

I also won't use the word *church*, even though translators of Paul commonly use it to render the Greek word *ekklēsia*. Similar problems are associated with this term. When we hear the word *church* today, we hear it as a term that applies specifically to *Christian* gatherings and buildings. Used in this way, *church* belongs to the same category as, but is distinct from, a synagogue or a mosque or a temple. It has been common from the early church fathers to modern theologians like Karl Barth to contrast the church and the synagogue, where the church stands for Christianity and the synagogue for Judaism.[3] But this is not what Paul or anyone reading one of Paul's letters in the first century would have thought when they heard him speak of an *ekklēsia*. The Greek word *ekklēsia* was simply a generic term that enjoyed widespread usage in the ancient Mediterranean world (both Jewish and non-Jewish) prior to the rise of the Jesus movement. For instance, in

---

3. E.g., Barth, *Church Dogmatics* I/1, 101.

ancient Athens it was used of the gathering of all the male citizens of the city. And it occurs one hundred times in the Septuagint, almost fifty times in Josephus, and almost twenty-five times in Philo. It simply means a gathering or an assembly of people. To translate this word as *church* when talking about Paul, then, is to give the term greater specificity than is appropriate, and it inevitably leads to thinking in more modern terms of Christians distinct from Jews. It would be like describing a group of birds in the distance with the word *banditry* (which can refer only to chickadees) or *murder* (which can refer only to crows), even though the type of bird being described is unverifiable. So I will use generic terms like *assembly* or *gathering* to translate *ekklēsia*.[4]

I will also avoid using the term *Christ*, which is merely an English transliteration of the Greek word *christos*, which means "anointed." Instead, I will regularly render *christos* as "Messiah" (itself a transliteration of the Hebrew) or, at times, "Anointed." The word *Christ*, I am convinced, is simply too familiar to modern readers and occludes the distinctly Jewish meaning of the word for Paul. We are too comfortable with speaking of Jesus as Christ without reflecting on the word's meanings. Admittedly we also are comfortable with speaking of Jesus as the Messiah, but whereas we speak of Jesus Christ regularly, almost as though Christ is Jesus's last name, we rarely speak of Jesus the Messiah. Messiah Jesus is slightly jarring to our ears, much as I think the honorific term *christos* would have been to Paul's first readers and hearers. It also stresses just how important Jewish messianism was to Paul's thinking. Jesus was a Jewish king for Paul, enthroned in his resurrection and ascension.[5]

Finally, English translators and commentators customarily speak of Paul the *apostle*, but this title is again nothing more than an English transliteration of the Greek word *apostolos*. *Apostle* does not communicate to English readers what the Greek would have in antiquity: someone sent on behalf of another person—a politically significant figure. It was used refer to ambassadors or envoys for a king, for

4. See Eyl, "Semantic Voids"; Korner, *Origin and Meaning of* Ekklēsia; and Kloppenborg, *Christ's Associations*.
5. See here Novenson, *Christ among the Messiahs*, and Jipp, *Christ Is King*.

instance. It could also have referred to a diplomatic and official role of one commissioned to speak on behalf of and to represent an important but absent person. So in this book I will speak of Paul as the Messiah's herald or envoy or ambassador. Paul depicts himself as one authorized—chosen and called—to serve as a spokesperson on behalf of a king: Jesus the Messiah.

I have discussed some words that I think confuse more than they clarify what Paul intends to say to his readers. But I still need to talk a bit about the method I use when studying Paul (or any ancient figure). The task of trying to re-create Paul's thinking is made difficult by the scant materials at hand. We have as few as twenty-four thousand words from his (or from his secretaries') stylus if we work only with the seven undisputed letters (Romans, 1–2 Corinthians, Galatians, Philippians, 1 Thessalonians, Philemon), and not much more even if we use all thirteen letters that bear his name. Imagine trying to distill everything that you believe in just fifty pages of typing. That might sound like a lot of space, but remember, you are trying to tell people *everything* you believe in a way that leads to no further questions or that results in no misunderstandings. It's an impossible task—not least of all because the fallibility of interpretation is inescapable.[6] But Paul wasn't even trying to do this. Rather, he wrote for particular people in specific places to address concrete issues within their communities. He wasn't writing for us, and he wasn't writing a systematic account of his thinking and theology. Not one letter, not even Romans, which Paul addresses to people who do not know him personally, seeks to be a complete distillation of his thought.

How are we today going to be able to summarize Paul's thinking when any honest account needs to grapple with the fact that there are gaps, some quite large, in what Paul writes? How do we deal with undeveloped and underdeveloped themes in what he says? And how do we weigh the things he does say when so much of it arises from a polemically charged location in response to specific issues? We could simply abandon the whole project, concluding that what Paul says

---

6. For an accessible account, see James K. A. Smith, *Fall of Interpretation*.

is occasional and spotty and perhaps of little theological value. Conversely, we could pretend that there is no issue at all and continue to treat his writings as an early systematic theology that can be read in a vacuum. In contrast to these two extremes, I think the historical method helps us reconstruct *some* of what remains hidden. Just as it would be silly to think that we could know how to translate words like *christos* or *ekklēsia* in Paul without looking at how other texts contemporaneous with Paul used these words, so too I think we cannot understand the broader claims Paul makes without situating him in what we can know about the first-century CE Mediterranean world, Jewish *and* non-Jewish.[7] In an important book on how to do history, John Lewis Gaddis argues that the work of the historian is in some ways parallel to the work of a paleontologist. Just as paleontologists use an incomplete fossil record to reconstruct what various species looked like or to map various evolutionary paths of life, so too historians necessarily fill in the fossil records, so to speak, of different figures and periods of history. In short, our work is "an exercise in historical paleontology."[8] This analogy applies to Paul. The question facing all readers of Paul, then, is this: How can one responsibly and meticulously excavate Paul's fragmentary literary fossils?

When it comes to the study of Paul, we have very few extant fossils: seven or so short and rhetorically charged letters. Such context-specific communications provide us with tiny windows into even tinier parts, various bones but not the entire skeleton, of Paul's thinking. How can historians make claims about what Paul thought or believed? Like paleontologists, Gaddis avers, "historians too start with surviving structures, whether they be archives, artifacts, or even memories. They then deduce the processes that produced them."[9] First, we are constrained to a certain degree by the way the words run on the

7. Engberg-Pedersen, *Paul in His Hellenistic Context*, and Engberg-Pedersen, *Paul Beyond the Judaism/Hellenism Divide*.
    8. Gaddis, *Landscape of History*, 42. I am indebted to Bert Harrill for drawing this work to my attention.
    9. Gaddis, *Landscape of History*, 41.

papyrus. Unfortunately, the written word is not particularly constrain-
ing. Already in Paul's own day, as I have noted, people understood
his writings in a multiplicity of ways, leading him to work to clarify
previous remarks, whether to those in Rome who heard his teaching
indirectly or to those in Corinth whose reception of his letters power-
fully demonstrates the difficulty inherent in the task of reading Paul.
As the Italian philosopher Umberto Eco has put it, "A text is a lazy
machinery which forces its possible readers to do a part of its textual
work."[10] Words on the papyrus place constraints on readers, but they
are weak and loose constraints: interpretative possibilities are not in-
finite, but they are also not singular. Nonetheless, as divided as the
field of Pauline studies is, we all agree that in writing letters to Rome
and Galatia, for instance, Paul did not intend his male readers to go
out and get circumcised (Gal. 5:2). The remains of Paul's writings tell
us this much, at least, about his mind and his intentions. But how can
we divine more nuanced aspects of Paul's mind, such as why Paul
did not want his male readers to get circumcised? It is here where
the readings of Paul that I discussed in the introduction part ways,
disagreeing over how to provide a historically plausible explanation
for Paul's imperatives not to get circumcised.

Here we return to methodology. To read Paul correctly, one must
place contextual constraints on his literary remains. One must not
only examine each bone carefully but also labor to locate those bones
within a broader web of other remains from Paul's geological stratum:
the broader ancient Mediterranean world, Jewish and non-Jewish.
When it comes to Paul, gentiles, and "Judaism," Terence Donaldson
has done considerable spadework in excavating and mapping out the
variegated nature of Jewish thinking about gentiles.[11] I think it im-
perative that we work to situate Paul, the self-proclaimed divinely appointed envoy of the Messiah to non-Jews, within the genus of Second
Temple Jewish thought, which was much more diverse than people
often recognize.[12] As Pamela Eisenbaum has argued, only when we

10. Eco, "Theory of Signs," 36.
11. Donaldson, *Judaism and the Gentiles*.
12. I have sought to do this in Thiessen, *Paul and the Gentile Problem*.

realize that "the teachings about Jewish law preserved in the apostle's letters are teachings about how Torah *is* and *is not* applicable to Gentiles, then Paul's reasoning begins to become clear."[13] For instance, it is simply wrong to believe that all or even most Second Temple Jews thought that gentiles needed to become Jews. Such a commonly held view is the result of Christian interpreters who have reconfigured Judaism into the image, albeit inevitably an inferior image, of Christianity. Since Christianity has historically required that others convert to it to experience God's deliverance, and because Christians have frequently missionized, so too Judaism must have required all people to become Jews to be saved.

But many Jews did not think that gentiles needed to convert, and very few Jews were in any way involved in activities that could be characterized as missionizing non-Jews.[14] So when Paul rejects the idea that gentiles can benefit from undergoing circumcision, he may be diverging from the position of some species of Jews who thought that gentiles could and should convert, but he is not breaking away from his genus, Judaism, and beginning his own path to a new genus, Christianity (at least not intentionally). Nonetheless, Paul's letters make up some of the raw materials that led, under the right combination of environmental conditions, to a genetic mutation in the early Jesus movement that caused it to evolve into something known as Christianity, a new movement categorized in part by what it was not: Judaism.

Admittedly, historical paleontology risks the danger of taking the bones of one species from the Second Temple period and wrongly using it for the reconstruction of the Pauline species. But if we refuse to use the bones of Paul's period, I do not think we will leave the Pauline skeleton riddled with holes. Instead, we will, unwittingly or otherwise, succumb to the temptation of supplying bones from different geological eras, most likely our own or, for many readers of Paul, those of the Reformation. We will use what is familiar and comfortable to us, and in so doing we will remake Paul in our image. But let's keep Paul weird!

13. Eisenbaum, *Paul Was Not a Christian*, 62.
14. See Wendt, *At the Temple Gates*.

Beyond this contextual work, Paul must be situated within yet another context: the historical context and the rhetorical purposes that led Paul to put stylus to papyrus. We must ask, Is it likely that Paul could have argued X? But we must also ask, How likely is it that Paul believed that he could convince others of X? In the words of Christopher Stanley, "It is Paul's persuasive intent that remains primary at every point, and the modern interpreter must read all that he says in the light of this concern or else risk misunderstanding."[15] We know that Paul wanted to convince his gentile readers that they stood to gain nothing from undergoing circumcision—his fossils tell us this much about his intentions. So our gap filling necessitates that we find some way to move from this intention to the way that the words run on the papyrus within the context of a period that contains other literary fossils that look the way that they do.

The more data we excavate and bring to bear on the study of Paul, whether for contextual or comparative purposes, the more likely we are going to read the remains of Paul accurately. This work can never be entirely objective, but it does place some constraints on readers. All historical work requires a degree of creativity and imagination. And in this creativity and imagination, we must acknowledge and take responsibility for our own choices. They are *choices*, and they are *ours*. And what we choose matters. Paula Fredriksen captures the tension here: "As historians, we conjure that innocence [that Paul had of the future] as a disciplined act of imagination, through appeals to our ancient evidence."[16] All reconstructions of Paul, from the longest Pauline theology (recall N. T. Wright's 1,700-page tome) to the briefest of articles, imaginatively construct a Paul, no matter how self-aware the writers are of this process. Margaret Mitchell has put it this way: "Pauline interpretation is fundamentally an artistic exercise in conjuring up and depicting a dead man from his ghostly images in the ancient text, as projected on a background composed from a selection of existing sources. All these portraits are based upon a new

15. Stanley, "'Under a Curse,'" 492.
16. Fredriksen, *Paul*, xii.

configuration of the surviving evidence, set into a particular, chosen, framework."[17] Engaging in artistic exercise . . . conjuring up . . . depicting . . . projecting on . . . composing from . . . selecting . . . choosing a framework. Each historian or exegete is the implied subject of these various actions, and each must accept responsibility for their actions.

I was trained in the methods of historical criticism as they relate to the study of ancient Judaism and Christianity. It has been (and still is!) difficult for me to come to terms with my own agency in reading Paul (or others). What feels like a *natural* way to study Paul, what feels like the *right* way to study Paul, is something specific to my social context and the unique history of biblical studies as a modern discipline.[18] There is a moral component to how one chooses to depict Paul, especially as one conjures this Paul in relation to Judaism. To minimize this fact or to claim that one is simply repeating what Paul says is to beg the question. All readers of Paul strive to depict him accurately, and yet we have competing accounts of him. I would argue that where uncertainty persists, we have a moral obligation to choose against readings that harm others. What I set out to do in the following pages is to provide a reading of Paul that is not dependent on the denigration of ancient Jews and Judaism. I do this because I think readings that do otherwise are historically implausible and, even more importantly, denigrate modern Jews and Judaism. Historically, Paul would have been surprised by the later Christian claim that he was rejecting Judaism and founding a new religion. And I think Paul would be dismayed at the way so much of Christian history and theology has been infected with a virulent form of anti-Judaism, that a movement that he helped shape has turned again and again to his writings to construct and fuel Christian anti-Judaism.

17. Mitchell, *Heavenly Trumpet*, 428.
18. Essential reading on whiteness and historical-critical approaches to biblical studies includes Parker, *If God Still Breathes*, and Horrell, *Ethnicity and Inclusion*. One can see a rich treatment of how African Americans have read Paul in Bowens, *African American Readings of Paul*.

2

A Radically New or a Long-Lost Reading of Paul?

I began this book with 2 Peter's assertion that Paul's letters are difficult to interpret correctly, but we have another early portrayal of Paul and his teachings in the Acts of the Apostles that makes a similar point.[1] Among other things, Acts of the Apostles is, to quote again Margaret Mitchell's words from the preceding chapter, an "artistic exercise in conjuring up and depicting [Paul]."[2] Acts never depicts Paul writing letters, mind you (not a particularly interesting thing to narrate after all), but it makes clear that Paul confused many of those who heard his teachings. The very shape

1. I have no desire to wade into the debates about when to date 2 Peter and Acts. Scholarly opinions range from the 60s to the 120s. On the face of it, that seems like a wide range, but when talking about texts that are almost two thousand years old, sixty years is the mere blink of an eye. Nothing in my arguments requires either an early or a late date to their composition.
2. Mitchell, *Heavenly Trumpet*, 428.

and order of the New Testament frames Paul's letters with statements about how they caused confusion early on.[3] A cursory reading of Paul's own letters shows that they confused people almost immediately. For instance, in Romans Paul seems to acknowledge that some have taken or might take his teaching as evidence that he advocates that people ought to continue to sin so that God's gift to them might increase (Rom. 6:2). And Paul needs to write to believers in Corinth to correct various misunderstandings they seem to have about what he initially wrote to them. And later someone had the audacity to write in the guise of Paul, in a work known as 3 Corinthians, to correct what *he* thought was a misunderstanding of Paul's words in 1 Corinthians 15.

Although 2 Peter does not identify which of Paul's statements confused readers, the Acts of the Apostles does. When readers get to Paul's final trip to Jerusalem, we learn that people there had been hearing some nasty rumors about what he was teaching Jews who lived outside Judea. The leaders of the Jesus movement in Jerusalem provide Paul with the following report: "You see, brother, how many thousands of believers there are among the Jews, and they are all zealous for the law. They have been told about you that you teach all the Jews living among the gentiles to forsake Moses and that you tell them not to circumcise their children or observe the customs" (Acts 21:20–21 NRSVue). These leaders tell Paul that they believe this report to be a set of malicious lies. They are certain that Paul does *not* teach Jews to give up the law and to stop circumcising their newborn baby boys. Obviously, somebody was getting Paul wrong. But who? There are only two options in the narrative world of Acts: either these rumors are true, or they aren't. Given these two options, it is obvious who is supposed to be right and who is supposed to be wrong in Luke's narrative: Luke assumes that the Jerusalem leaders, who are among his

---

3. Nienhuis and Wall, *Reading the Epistles*, 34: "The decision to embrace Paul's writings with the Acts of the Apostles on one side and the [Catholic Epistles (i.e., James, 1–2 Peter, Jude, 1–3 John)] on the other appears attributable to the overriding theological concern that Paul be interpreted *within* the particular theological framework afforded by Acts and the [Catholic Epistles]. Paul is thus handed down to us in the full embrace of his apostolic colleagues." Cf. Nienhuis, *Not by Paul Alone*.

heroes, have correctly understood Paul's message. *For Luke*, the claim that Paul teaches Jewish people who live among gentiles that they should abandon Moses, leaving their sons uncircumcised and giving up observing the Jewish law, is simply false.

The Jerusalem leaders discuss how best to dispel this misunderstanding about Paul and come up with a seemingly simple solution: four Jewish followers of Jesus had recently come to Jerusalem and were currently under a Nazirite vow. Since they were about to go through the rite of ritual purification required by the law (Num. 6), Paul should be purified with them and pay for their heads to be shaved to signal the completion of both their and his Nazirite vows since Paul took the same vow earlier in the narrative (Acts 18:18). When Paul performs this set of actions in a very public way in the Jerusalem temple, "all will know that there is nothing in what they have been told about you but that you yourself observe and guard the law" (Acts 21:23–24 NRSVue).

The brevity of this story belies its importance, both for what it tells us about Luke and for what it says about Luke's Paul. Given the anti-legalistic, anti-ethnocentric, and apocalyptic accounts of Paul, one would expect Paul to stand up to the Jerusalem leaders in much the same way that he seems to stand up to Peter in Antioch (Gal. 2). The anti-legalistic reading seems to require Paul to declare that neither Jews nor gentiles are saved by works and so Jews do not need to keep the law and no longer need to circumcise their sons. This Paul should then tell the Jerusalem leaders that he will not take part in cultic practices that make him appear to be law observant, since doing so would be bearing false testimony. The anti-ethnocentric reading appears to require Paul to declare to the Jerusalem leaders that their insistence on law observance and their contention that ethnicity matters are idolatrous and ethnocentric. Again, this Paul should resist the call to participate in the Jerusalem cult since to do so would be to suggest that Jewish distinctives like circumcision, purity regulations, and the temple (works of the law) still matter. And the apocalyptic reading seems to require Paul to declare that the old has passed in light of the apocalyptic invasion of the Messiah: the temple, ritual purity regulations, and ethnicity are all nothing in the wake of the messianic new creation.

But Luke's Paul does none of these things. Instead, he does precisely what is asked of him, knowing full well that it will give and is *intended* to give everyone the impression that he himself keeps the Jewish law. These publicly performed rituals show people that Paul was not teaching Jewish Messiah followers outside Judea to abandon Moses, the Jewish rite of circumcision, or the Jewish law. The story makes clear that ethnic distinctions persist and matter in the Jesus movement: one set of practices applies to Jewish followers of Jesus, while another set of practices applies to gentile followers of Jesus (Acts 21:25). Laws, ethnicity, and differences continue to matter for Luke's Paul.

But what are we to make of this depiction of Paul in Acts 21? Either the Paul in the narrative world of Acts (note please, I am not yet talking about the "historical Paul") really did expect Jewish Messiah followers to keep the law and did so himself, and so his actions here are consistent with his thinking and behavior, or Paul taught Jewish Messiah followers to abandon Moses, circumcision, and the Jewish law (and did so himself), and so his actions here are wildly misleading, deceitful even, and utterly hypocritical. It is hardly likely that Luke, who portrays Paul as one of the key leaders of a movement he thinks is God's work, would depict Paul as untrustworthy. In Luke's mind, Paul is no liar. Luke's Paul is no hypocrite. Luke's Paul insists on law observance both for himself and for other Jewish followers of Jesus.

Elsewhere in Acts Paul claims to be a Jew faithful to God, his people, and the Jewish law. In his discussion with Festus, the new Roman governor of Judea, he declares, "I have in no way [sinned; Greek: *hēmarton*] against the law of the Jews or against the temple or against the emperor" (25:8 NRSVue). And in the final chapter of Acts, when Paul is imprisoned in Rome, he tells the Jewish residents of the city, "Brothers, . . . I had done nothing against our people or the customs of our ancestors" (28:17 NRSVue). Again, we have two options regarding Paul's claims within the context of Luke's narrative. Either his claims

are true, or they are not. Perhaps, being on trial for his very life, Paul
lied to save himself. While one could hardly blame a person for lying
to save their own skin, nothing within the narrative of Acts suggests
that Luke believes this to be the case with Paul. As Kavin Rowe has argued, "For Luke, Paul is a 'reliable' character; indeed, he is the human
protagonist of much of Acts. Thus does Paul's declaration offer an interpretive guide to the entirety of the trial and to his appearance before
Roman officials."[4] Luke intentionally depicts Paul as a law-observant
Jewish follower of Jesus until the very end, one who *did not* teach Jewish Messiah followers to abandon the law of Moses and one who did
not oppose the Jewish law.

Consequently, we are left with another problem, now one related
to the historical Paul and not merely the narrative world of Acts. If
the Paul we can learn about from Paul's letters does not keep the Jewish law, and if he teaches Messiah followers, including Jewish Messiah followers, to abandon the law of Moses and circumcision, then
Luke's depiction contradicts the historical Paul. Has Luke himself
misunderstood Paul? Surely it is possible that Luke has mistakenly
misrepresented Paul, his actions, and his thinking in the narrative of
Acts. Or maybe Luke hasn't misunderstood Paul at all but has *chosen*
to misrepresent Paul to others. Either way, this is no small distortion.
It would be akin, for instance, to a biographer claiming that Bernie
Sanders, an American politician who identifies as a Democratic Socialist, is a card-carrying member of the Libertarian Party. These
two political positions are antithetical to one another. The claim that
Bernie is a Libertarian is irreconcilable with the claim that he is a
Democratic Socialist. Both simply cannot be true. And to confuse
one with the other would be both inaccurate and offensive—Bernie
would no doubt disagree vehemently with anyone who claims that he
is a Libertarian. So too with the historical Paul. Traditional accounts
of Paul understand him to be strongly opposed to the observance
of the Jewish law, both for Jewish and for gentile Messiah followers. To depict him as law observant is to contradict these common

4. Rowe, *World Upside Down*, 80.

accounts. If Luke is *this* wrong about Paul, then surely he falls under the condemnation of 2 Peter 3:16, showing himself to be "ignorant and unstable," someone who twists Paul's words to "their own destruction" (NRSVue).

So modern readers of Paul are left with a choice. Side with common and traditional accounts of Paul against Luke, or side with Luke against traditional accounts of Paul. For the scholar of religion and the historian, either of these choices presents no methodological problem—one must simply weigh the evidence of Paul's letters, and if Luke is wrong, so be it. But for readers who view these texts as scripture, I would argue that this choice is not really any choice at all. Should one side with so-called traditional readings of Paul against the *canonical* text of Acts? Should the Acts of the Apostles be any less authoritative than Paul's writings?

I am convinced that the shape of the *Christian* canon ought to dictate how *Christian* readers interpret Paul's letters. While the New Testament underwent shaping and formation, Christians eventually decided on a canon in which the Acts of the Apostles was placed right before the letters of Paul.[5] As such, Acts introduces the reader to Paul. Before one even gets to any of his letters, one learns that Paul has been misunderstood in relation to the Jewish law. Luke wants to give his readers the key to getting Paul right, and whatever their precise intentions, those who established the form of the New Testament canon did so as well. This is how Acts functions within the canon: it is the authoritative interpretation of Paul, meant to keep people from misreading and misusing Paul's letters. I think it provides Christian readers, at the very least, with the key to unlocking Paul, especially as he relates to the Judaism(s) of his day. Acts, then, helps not just with Paul but also with modern theological questions of supersessionism and the relationship between Judaism and Christianity.[6]

---

5. The evidence is helpfully collected in Gallagher and Meade, *Biblical Canon Lists*.

6. For a late medieval Jewish reading of Acts that is in line with my reading here, see Profiat Duran's *Shame of the Gentiles*, which has been translated into English and analyzed in Berlin, "Shame of the Gentiles of Profiat Duran."

Lest anyone conclude that we must allow Luke's account of Paul to override the evidence of what Paul himself wrote, I suggest that Paul's own letters point in this direction, *when properly read*. I will turn to this argument shortly, but let me add that Luke's reading of Paul also helps strengthen the inner coherence of the Christian canon as a whole. How does one go from a law-observant Jesus in the Gospels to a Paul who abolishes the law in Paul's letters?[7] Perhaps Luke's depiction of Paul better connects Jesus and Paul. For that matter, how can one make sense of the traditional Paul in relation to the many commandments God gives to Israel in what Christians refer to as the Old Testament? Does Paul disagree with and reject key parts of Jewish scriptures? Does he believe that there is some fundamental disagreement or contradiction or tension within his sacred texts?[8]

Ironically, one place where most interpreters have understood Paul to disagree explicitly with Jewish scriptures is, I am convinced, the internal key for unlocking how to read Paul's letters with regard to this messianic movement and the Jewish law. In his letter to Messiah followers living in Corinth, Paul addresses the question of sex and marriage. Those in Corinth had written Paul, apparently concluding that it was good for Messiah followers not to have sex (1 Cor. 7:1). My hunch is that this claim seemed like the natural conclusion to Paul's teaching that Messiah followers have become living temples of the holy *pneuma* (often translated as "Spirit"—more on this later). Since both Jews and non-Jews commonly believed one became ritually impure through sex and could not enter into holy space for a short period of time afterward, it only made sense that, if one's own body was an actual temple, one must distance that temple from sexual activity.[9] Paul disagrees, suggesting that married Messiah followers should

7. Yes, this remains a controversial claim. It should not be. See my *Jesus and the Forces of Death*.

8. Such is the argument of Watson, *Paul and the Hermeneutics of Faith*, 23: "In reading the Torah, Paul chooses to highlight two major tensions that he finds within it: the tension between the unconditional promise and the Sinai legislation, and the tension between the law's offer of life and its curse. These are tensions between *books*: Genesis, Exodus, Leviticus and Deuteronomy."

9. On human bodies functioning as sacred space, see Harrington, *Purity and Sanctuary of the Body*.

have sex, even though it creates *ritual* impurity, so that they do not give in to lust, *moral* impurity. He then turns to unmarried people and widows, telling them not to seek out marriage unless they really cannot control their lust. (Sorry, but Paul was hardly a romantic.) Similarly, Paul wants all married people to remain in the state of marriage, even those married to unbelievers, if possible. He then provides his reason for his positions: "Let each of you lead the life that the Lord has assigned, in which God called you. This is what I demand in all the assemblies" (1 Cor. 7:17). This is Paul's ruling principle, he claims, in all the various groups of Messiah followers he has organized. While Paul's letters are occasional, directed to different situations in different cities, one of his consistent maxims is that believers are to remain as they are. He repeats this rule in 1 Corinthians 7:20: "Let each of you remain in the calling in which you were called." In between these two pronouncements, Paul provides an example to illustrate how this rule should be applied to the rite of circumcision: "Was anyone at the time of his call already circumcised? Let him not seek epispasm [a medical procedure that resulted in the regrowth of the circumcised foreskin]. Was anyone at the time of his call foreskinned?[10] Let him not undergo circumcision" (7:18). He then makes what appears to be an audacious claim: "Neither the circumcision is anything, nor is the foreskin anything, but keeping the commandments of God" (7:19).

Most readers have understood Paul here to be saying that circumcision no longer matters because it is no longer (or perhaps never was) one of God's commandments. Such an assertion would fly in the face of the claims of Jewish scriptures, which assert that God commanded Israel to practice the rite of circumcision on their newborn male children throughout their generations (Gen. 17:9–14; Lev. 12:3). How can this be? Has Paul concluded that these passages wrongly attribute the rite of circumcision to God when it was merely human-made custom? Nowhere else does Paul suggest that any aspect of the

---

10. While it is common to translate the Greek work *akrobystia* as "uncircumcised," the word means "foreskin" or "foreskinned." Cf. Neutel, "Restoring Abraham's Foreskin."

Jewish law is of human, not divine, origin. Elsewhere he even says that "the law is holy, and the commandment is holy and just and good" (Rom. 7:12 NRSVue). And to the question of what value the rite of circumcision has, Paul answers, "Much, in every way" (Rom. 3:1–2 NRSVue).

So what does Paul mean in 1 Corinthians 7:19? N. T. Wright describes this verse as being "almost Zen-like in its density of redefinition."[11] That is, Wright believes Paul has redefined what the commandments of God are so that they no longer include the central commandment to Israel to practice circumcision. Unsurprisingly Wright appears to have little problem with this type of redefinition. Most Christians through the centuries, after all, have happily redefined what circumcision refers to in order to avoid any potential suggestion that physical circumcision might still be relevant for Paul and therefore for readers of Paul. But most (maybe all?) ancient Jews would have found such a redefinition to be perplexing at best and offensive at worst. Consider a modern example. Were some Christian preacher to claim that baptism or communion had no value and that the audience should only listen to God's words, wouldn't most Christians respond by simply pointing to the passages in the Christian Bible that affirm the importance of these central rites? How convincing would such a claim be to those listening to this preacher?[12] This reading of Paul is, to my mind, historically implausible and rhetorically unpersuasive.

Instead, Paul *does* think that circumcision matters because he tells people in Galatia that if they undergo circumcision, it will adversely affect them: "Listen! I, Paul, am telling you that, if you let yourselves be circumcised, the Messiah will be of no benefit to you" (Gal. 5:2 NRSVue alt.). If the common reading of 1 Corinthians 7:19 is correct, then it contradicts Paul's claim in Galatians 5:2. While it is possible that Paul changed his mind, the reality is that he makes a similar claim, using virtually the same language as 1 Corinthians 7:19, in his letter to Galatia: "For neither circumcision is anything,

---

11. Wright, *Paul and the Faithfulness of God*, 361.
12. This, of course, isn't merely hypothetical since neither Quakers nor the Salvation Army practice baptism or communion.

nor is foreskin anything, but a new creation" (Gal. 6:15). He has already made a claim akin to this, with slightly different wording, only
four verses after his claim that getting circumcised would have detrimental consequences for the Galatians: "For in the Messiah Jesus
neither circumcision nor foreskin has strength, but faith working
through love" (5:6).[13]

What, then, could Paul mean when he contrasts circumcision and
foreskin to the commandments of God? I think the answer is quite
simple: the phrases "the circumcision" and "the foreskin" refer to
two groups of people: circumcised Jews and foreskinned gentiles.
We have clear and early evidence that people within Messiah groups
connected to Paul used these two terms in rhetorically and ethnically
charged ways to refer to each other. Ephesians, whether Paul wrote
this letter or not, makes this apparent when its author reminds gentile readers that they are called "foreskin" by those who are, in turn,
called "circumcision" (2:11). And Paul uses these terms to refer to
gentiles and Jews, claiming that Israel's God has given him the good
news of the foreskin, while to Peter, God has given the good news
of the circumcision (Gal. 2:7). The *of* in these two phrases (the good
news *of* the foreskin and the good news *of* the circumcision) does
not mean that the content of Paul's message is about the foreskin or
that the content of Peter's message is about the rite of circumcision.[14]
Rather, the *of* signifies the audience of their respective messages.
In the very next verse Paul continues to use *the circumcision* for the
audience of Peter's good news, while he switches to *the gentiles* for
the audience of his good news (Gal. 2:8). The title *the foreskin*, then, is
interchangeable in Paul's mind with the phrase *the gentiles*.[15] (Modern
Christians are no doubt grateful that these indelicate names didn't
stick!)

Returning to 1 Corinthians 7:18–19, then, Paul advises his readers to remain in the state in which God called them. If you are foreskinned, stay foreskinned. If you are circumcised, stay circumcised.

13. See Sanfridson, "Are Circumcision and Foreskin *Really* Nothing?"
14. Collman, *Apostle to the Foreskin.*
15. For more, see Marcus, "Circumcision and the Uncircumcision in Rome."

Why? Because, for the purposes of God's saving acts, it does not matter if one is a Jew or a gentile, the circumcision or the foreskin. But for the purposes of behavior, it does matter if one is a Jew or a gentile. What matters is keeping the commandments that God has placed on a person in the state when God first called them. If one is a Jew, there are commandments that apply to Jewish followers of the Messiah. If one is a gentile, there are certain commandments that apply to gentile followers of the Messiah. For eschatological deliverance, ethnicity does not matter in the Messiah. But for behavior, ethnicity continues to matter in the Messiah. This interpretation of 1 Corinthians 7:18-19 fits hand in glove with the depiction of Paul in Acts 21.

Paul's letters are occasional—they are directed to specific people who lived in a specific place at a specific time in specific circumstances. But at least in this passage, Paul suggests that the circumstances and geography and people that differ from letter to letter do not matter. This is Paul's universal rule for Messiah followers: remain in the state in which you were called. To be sure, part of this rule depends on the circumstances: Paul thinks he and all Messiah followers face the nearing eschatological climax to human history. But the rule stands. If a person is a Jewish follower of the Messiah, they should continue to be a Jewish follower of the Messiah. Do not try to change that identity now. If someone is a gentile follower of the Messiah, they also should not try to change that identity. What this means is that Jewish followers of Jesus should not abandon their ancestral customs in an effort to act or become more like gentiles. Likewise, gentile followers of Jesus should not undergo circumcision in the hope that they might act more like or even become Jews. God's commandments, distinct for Jews and for gentiles, still matter. What does not matter in relation to God's saving work is whether one is a Jew or a gentile. As Paul tells his readers in Galatia, in the Messiah there is neither Jew nor Greek (Gal. 3:28). Being Jewish or being gentile, belonging to the circumcision or to the foreskin, is important but only incidental to God's deliverance. God saves both. To attempt to change one's identity implies, whether the person realizes it or not, that God saves only Jews and so gentiles need to

Judaize themselves, or that God saves only gentiles and so Jews need to gentilize themselves.

To require others to change their ethnic identity or to desire to change one's own ethnic identity, then, makes a larger theological statement about Israel's God. Such changed behavior in the hope of changing one's ethnic identity implies that God is the God of one ethnic group but not the other. This goes both ways. Christian interpreters have for a long time recognized that one of the reasons Paul so vehemently condemns efforts to turn gentiles into Jews is that it would then imply that God is the God of the Jews only: "Or is God the God of Jews only? Is he not the God of gentiles also? Yes, of gentiles also" (Rom. 3:29 NRSVue). The anti-ethnocentric reading of Paul is right, therefore, in stressing that one of Paul's problems with how certain people were using the Jewish law was that gentiles were hearing that to be acceptable to God they needed to become Jews. But the anti-ethnocentric reading of Paul is only half of the theological story. There is an unstated but logical corollary in Romans 3, unstated because it was unnecessary in Paul's day, but it has been necessary for Christians to hear for the subsequent two thousand years of history and thinking. Had Paul been aware of Jews who were abandoning their ancestral customs in an effort to become gentile followers of the Messiah, he would have vehemently rejected this action. His words would then have read: "Or is God the God of the gentiles only? Is God not the God of the Jews also? Yes, of the Jews also!" Remain in the state in which God called you. In other words, one's ethnic identity as a Jew or a gentile is an integral part of God's calling and God's plan of deliverance. To attempt to change your ethnic identity would be to suggest that God can't save you as you are. And it is here where the anti-legalistic reading of Paul gets something fundamentally correct as well: God's saving acts are for both Jew and gentile and are not contingent on whatever works one is capable of doing.

We have looked at two clues for how to read Paul: one external (the depiction of Paul in Acts of the Apostles) and one internal (Paul's own universal rule in 1 Cor. 7:19). One provides early reception-historical, theological, and canonical support to the reading I will give in the fol-

lowing pages, while the other provides internal and therefore historical support for this reading: a law-observant Paul who follows Jesus
the Messiah. In short, a Jewish Paul. Not an anomalous Jew, not a radical Jew, not a marginal Jew. Just one Jew living his life and following
his perceived calling amid the diversity and richness of first-century
Judaism.

3

Judaism Doesn't Believe Anything

Judaism doesn't believe anything, but Jews do. Judaism doesn't teach anything. But Jews do. Judaism doesn't do anything. But Jews do. Judaism doesn't have a mind to think or a voice to speak or a body to act. But Jews do. When we speak of Judaism (or Christianity or Hinduism or Islam or atheism), we are using an abstraction. As Paula Fredriksen puts it, "The *-ism* of 'Judaism' implies broad, abstract and articulated trans-local ideological consensus, but in point of fact—then as now—vigorously various *enactments* of Jewishness prevailed."[1] Judaism is a name that collects all individual Jews and puts them into one category. And doing so almost inevitably leads to generalizations and oversimplification. Whenever you hear the claim that "Judaism believed X," you should immediately question whether this was indeed the case, because it implies that *all* Jews believed X.

1. Fredriksen, "*Al Tirah* ('Fear Not!')," 29.

A contemporary example: Canada is such a polite country. This is a generalization people make based on a limited experience of Canadian people. But does this mean that all Canadians are unfailingly polite? As a Canadian, I can assure you that this stereotype applies to *some* Canadians—definitely not to all of us. But when a Canadian is not being polite, does that mean they are no longer Canadian? Surely not. And not all of us play hockey or curl or enjoy winter or are lumberjacks. Is a Canadian less Canadian if they, like me, hate winter and are at serious risk of broken bones if they lace up a pair of skates? Of course not. The same danger lurks in claiming that Judaism believed X or did Y; it might lead people to think that if a particular Jew does not do X or Y, that Jew is a bad Jew or has ceased to be a Jew altogether.

Who gets to decide who is a Jew and who isn't? Who gets to decide what constitutes good Jewish behavior or bad Jewish behavior or true Jewish belief and false Jewish belief? After all, there was (and is) no Jewish equivalent to the pope. In this regard, Jews are more similar to Mennonites than they are to Roman Catholics. The figure of Moses comes closest to a pope-like figure, but in the first century CE different Jewish leaders and interpreters of Moses existed: the high priest, the Jerusalem priests, the Sanhedrin (a council of Jewish leaders), and the Herodian dynasty, to name a few. The Essenes had their Teacher of Righteousness. Others followed John the Baptizer. Within the movement of the Pharisees, some appealed to Rabbi Hillel, while others appealed to Rabbi Shammai. And another group followed a Galilean teacher named Jesus. None of these figures was universally perceived to be the final, authoritative voice for Jews or Judaism, like the pope is for Catholics.[2]

If Christians heard a religious studies professor claim that Christians baptize their children as infants, most would realize that this is an inaccurate generalization. Major streams of Christianity do baptize infants (e.g., Roman Catholics, Eastern Orthodox, Anglican), but many other Christians baptize only older youth and adults (e.g., Mennonites,

2. Anyone paying attention to Roman Catholicism knows that even the pope does not enjoy unquestioned authority among all Catholics. Pope Benedict had detractors among certain Catholics, while Pope Francis has his among other Catholics.

Baptists, Pentecostals) and do so upon their verbal confession of faith. We all know about some of the diversity of beliefs and behaviors that exist within our own religious or political traditions and rightly balk at claims that seem ignorant of this diversity—especially when that ignorance results in a derogatory or demeaning generalization. We want others to talk about us and our people, however defined, with precision, care, and sympathy. We should extend that same sympathy and sensitivity toward others, questioning any claims that reduce other religious traditions to some overly simplistic and inaccurate unity.

Realizing this is fundamental to thinking about ancient Judaism in general and then thinking about Paul in relation to his fellow Jews. Ancient Jews were not a monolithic group in what they thought and believed or in how they acted. We know this already from the evidence of the New Testament. The Sadducees, for instance, did not believe in the resurrection, something many other Jews hoped for. According to Acts 23:6–10, Paul used this inner-Jewish disagreement in his defense to great rhetorical and judicial effect. And the first-century Jewish historian Josephus mentions three groups in Judea: the Pharisees, the Sadducees, and the Essenes.[3] We know, then, of at least five distinct groups of Jews in Judea alone: followers of John the Immerser, Jesus followers, Pharisees, Sadducees, and Essenes. To complicate matters, Luke claims that these weren't always distinct groups since there were Pharisees who believed in Jesus (Acts 15:5; cf. John 3). And Luke depicts Paul still claiming to be a Pharisee (Acts 23:6; 26:5). For that matter, most Jews in the first century likely weren't card-carrying members of any particular group.

Some Jews believed in the existence of angels, and others did not (again, Sadducees). Some Jews believed that the Jerusalem temple was functioning properly, others thought it had been fundamentally misused and needed to be reinstituted (the Qumran community), and other people related to but distinct from Jews thought it was located at the wrong place (Samaritans). Some Jews believed you absolutely needed to circumcise your sons on the eighth day after they were

3. Klawans, *Josephus and the Theologies of Ancient Judaism.*

born (see the book of Jubilees), while others thought you had a bit of leeway under extenuating circumstances (many rabbis). In the second century CE, some Jews believed that a man by the name of Simon bar Kosiba was the Messiah, and others did not. And some Jews believed that a Galilean man named Jesus was the Messiah, and others did not.

Beyond the question of a founding figure or an authoritative interpreter of sacred texts, Jews did not even agree completely on which texts were authoritative and which were not. Moving beyond the Five Books of Moses was bound to initiate vigorous debate.[4] It is not my intention to catalog all the ways in which Jews disagreed with one another in antiquity, in terms of both beliefs and actions, but I wish to give readers a sense of these disagreements, especially about such major questions as what texts were authoritative or what, if anything, the afterlife looked like.[5]

Paul's Former Way of Life

Once we recognize that ancient Judaism was very diverse, we can begin to see some of the false assumptions that we might entertain about Jesus and Paul and about the rise of what, at some point, became Christianity.[6] If Jews held different opinions about many (if not all) topics, and if Jews lived out their identities differently from one another, then we cannot know with any certainty that Paul's belief about this topic or that practice meant that he broke away from Judaism. Think about the statement Paul makes about his life before Jesus is revealed to him, as the NRSVue translates it, "You have heard, no doubt, of my earlier life in Judaism. I was violently persecuting the church of God and was trying to destroy it. I advanced in Judaism beyond many among my

---

4. Again, Christians are not dissimilar, given the different Christian canons that exist to this day—Protestant, Roman Catholic, and various Orthodox canons.

5. Even someone as sensitive to the details of ancient Judaism as E. P. Sanders (*Judaism: Practice and Belief*) can be guilty of making ancient Jews appear more monolithic than they actually were.

6. On the tricky question of when Christianity became something distinct from Judaism, see Becker and Reed, *Ways That Never Parted*, and Baron, Hicks-Keeton, and Thiessen, *Ways That Often Parted*.

people of the same age, for I was far more zealous for the traditions of my ancestors" (Gal. 1:13–14).

Many interpreters have taken these verses to demonstrate that Paul had abandoned the religion of Judaism. Given what the NRSVue and other modern translations do with Paul's Greek here, I don't blame them. First, remember that *ekklēsia* means not "church" but an "assembly," here a group of Jesus followers. Beyond that, what would it have looked like for Paul to abandon Judaism? Was he kicked out of Judaism? If so, by whom? Or did he come to believe that he had left Judaism regardless of what others thought? Did Paul believe that he had come to be something other than and mutually exclusive of a Jew? Is Paul here saying he is no longer a Jew but a Christian? Remember, Christianity did not exist, so Paul couldn't have abandoned Judaism for Christianity. And Paul never uses the term *Christian*, either because he didn't know it or because he didn't like it. Did Paul quit Judaism and being a Jew?

Apparently not. Only a few sentences later Paul calls himself (and Peter) a Jew (Gal. 2:15). As Pamela Eisenbaum notes, "It is very important to stress that Paul does not use the designation 'Jew' of himself as a label of his religious past."[7] Elsewhere, he refers to his Benjaminite identity and his Israelite identity (Rom. 11:1; Phil. 3:5).[8] And he still holds to many things that are distinctively and exclusively (at the time) Jewish. He cites various Jewish scriptures as though they are sacred and authoritative. His god is the God of the Jews (Rom. 3:1, 29). And he follows Jesus, whom he believes is Israel's Messiah, a Jewish eschatological figure. So how could Paul have left something called Judaism if he still held to all these Jewish things?

In contrast to many interpreters, I take Paul's claim in Galatians 1:13–14 to mean that he had abandoned one form of what we might call Judaism, a particular form shaped by the traditions of the Pharisees, for another form of what we might call Judaism, a form shaped by a distinctive belief that Israel's God had already sent Israel's Messiah,

7. Eisenbaum, *Paul Was Not a Christian*, 6.
8. For one recent effort to grapple with the titles *Jew* and *Israelite* and how they relate and differ from one another, see Staples, *Idea of Israel in Second Temple Judaism*.

identified as the crucified man Jesus, whom Paul believed Israel's God
had raised from the dead. That is, God had *resurrected* him, a Jewish
eschatological belief pertaining to the righteous dead. In other words,
what Paul had undergone is much closer to what modern religious
people might see as changing denominations, not changing religions.
It's more like a Reform Jew becoming an Orthodox Jew, or a Baptist
becoming a Roman Catholic. But even this comparison has its limits
because, for Paul, the central questions have to do with Jesus's identity
as the Messiah and what time it is in God's eschatological scheme.
Such a change in life no doubt angered and offended some of Paul's
Jewish contemporaries, but not because they thought he had abandoned something called Judaism and had ceased to be a Jew. That Paul
received thirty-nine lashes at the hands of some of his fellow Jews on
five separate occasions (2 Cor. 11:24; cf. Deut. 25:2–3) suggests that they
believed he fell within the bounds of Judaism and required corporal
discipline in order to restore him to what they believed to be faithful
Jewish practice. That he experienced these lashings on multiple occasions suggests that he continued to live and move within Jewish circles.
Paul did not cease to be a Jew, either in his mind or in the minds of
others, even those who disagreed with him. Rather, Paul had become
a messianic Jewish follower of Jesus. For some, this change meant
that Paul had become a bad or a misguided Jew. For Paul, this change
meant that he was being faithful to the eschatological revelation of
God's son, the Messiah (Gal. 1:15–16).

Jewish Diversity and Gentiles

The common error of thinking about Judaism in monolithic terms
applies to a central topic for my approach to Paul: the relationship between gentiles, Israel, and Israel's God. When modern readers of Paul
think about Judaism, they often think about Judaism in distinctively
Christian terms. This is natural, albeit regrettable. When we encounter
something new or unfamiliar, it is easy to "translate" it for ourselves
by relating it to things we know well. For example, one of the first

friends my daughter made in kindergarten was Jewish. My daughter frequently came home fascinated by the different practices of her friend, but she would seek to translate those practices into ones that were more familiar to her. Her friend's family would go to synagogue, which my daughter called their "church." She celebrated Hanukkah, which my daughter thought of as "Jewish Christmas," because of the time of year and the food, gifts, and lights. What is understandable in a child (even as we sought to correct her gently) is unhelpful in historical and religious studies. It is also unhelpful in ecumenical contexts. Since virtually all readers of Paul's letters have been Christian (until the rise of the academic study of religion over the last century or so),[9] they almost automatically compare Judaism to Christianity. This is a mistake for several reasons and is unfair to Judaism, which, after all, was not and is not trying to be Christianity.[10]

One of the most common ways in which people mistakenly think about Judaism in Christian categories, especially in relation to Paul, involves ideas about conversion and missionizing. For many Christians, one's faith requires one to share that faith with others. If Christianity is true, and if eschatological deliverance is found in Jesus alone, then one should *want* others to come to faith in Jesus. And if you are saved only by Jesus, isn't there a moral obligation for his followers to make that message known to the world and to everyone, regardless of ethnicity, regardless of where they live, and regardless of what religions they currently subscribe to?

I recall as a child hearing the following about the need to evangelize friends, neighbors, and ultimately, the world: Imagine yourself on the *Titanic*. You are enjoying your evening dinner and the music that fills the dining room. The night is perfect and promises to be memorable until an uncouth worker storms into the dining hall and yells out, "The *Titanic* has hit an iceberg and is sinking! Everyone needs to board one

9. For Jewish interactions with Paul, see Langton, *Apostle Paul in the Jewish Imagination*.

10. Even among those who seek to study religion from a more neutral position, this is a frequent problem and one that is indebted to the peculiarly Christian origins and institutional contexts of the academic study of religion. On the problem of comparative religious studies in general, see the work of Jonathan Z. Smith, especially *Drudgery Divine*, and Masuzawa, *Invention of World Religions*.

of the lifeboats! If you don't, you will die!" You, eating your dinner and listening to music, will not view this message as good news. You will not welcome the disruption of your gilded evening. You will not be pleased to hear that a lovely night has turned into a life-threatening catastrophe. But ultimately, if the *Titanic* is sinking, you're glad someone told you so that you can be saved. So too, many Christians believe that they have a moral obligation to tell people throughout the world that they are doomed and that they need the lifeboat, so to speak, of Jesus so that they do not drown (or burn) in the lake of fire. For these Christians, the *only* lifeboat for everyone is Jesus, so everyone needs to board this vessel—Christianity—to be saved. Beyond a moral obligation, if you fear that your loved ones or your fellow humans are doomed to eternal torment unless they come to faith in Jesus, your own humanity and love and compassion might compel you to share your faith with others.[11]

Christians who hold such a view (and not all do) often think that other religions must believe something similar. As a result, many readers of Paul, scholars and otherwise, have depicted Judaism as a religion that seeks to provide a path to heaven, off the sinking ship on which all humanity—Jews and non-Jews—lives. But this was not generally the case in the ancient world, nor is it the case today. For many ancient Jews, a person did not need to be a Jew for Israel's God to save them.[12] Consequently, Jews rarely, if ever, sought to missionize non-Jews. And the few instances where we see Jews encouraging non-Jews to adopt Jewish customs do not provide evidence of a widespread missionary impulse within Judaism that sought to save people from hell or damnation; instead, they are instances of the larger phenomenon of what both Ronald Charles and Heidi Wendt have called "itinerant freelance religious expertise."[13]

There may have been a few Jews who believed that, to be saved, non-Jews needed to undergo conversion and become Jews themselves.

11. For one theological attempt to undermine this whole way of thinking, see Hart, *That All Shall Be Saved*.
12. See the epilogue, for instance, to Boyarin, *Radical Jew*.
13. The full phrase comes from Wendt, *At the Temple Gates*, but Charles (*Paul and the Politics of Diaspora*, 249) anticipates it in his language of a "first-century Jewish itinerant Diaspora figure."

But evidence for such a position is exceedingly limited. Two of the strongest pieces of evidence appear in the New Testament: the Gospel of Matthew, which depicts Jesus lambasting the Pharisees for going to great lengths to make one proselyte (23:15), and Acts, which connects certain Pharisees to the idea that gentiles need to adopt circumcision (for men) and other Jewish practices to be saved (15:1, 5). With regard to Matthew, Jesus's saying here may refer not to the religious conversion of *gentiles* but to the efforts of the Pharisees to convince other *Jews* to join their particular interpretation of what faithful Jewish practices should be.[14] I am not persuaded by this reading of the verse, but if it is correct, then it points to a Pharisaic practice that is akin to Baptists missionizing Catholics. Outside of these two texts, Josephus mentions a Jewish man named Eleazar, likely also a Pharisee, who tells a gentile ruler named Izates that there is no point in reading Jewish scriptures unless one commits to doing what these scriptures command, including undergoing circumcision.[15] So Matthew, Acts, and Josephus all connect these isolated Jewish efforts to missionize and convert non-Jews to Jewish customs to the Pharisees (more on this in the next chapter).

But if our sources are representative, missionizing of non-Jews was unusual. Far more common was a live-and-let-live approach to gentiles. Israel's God was also the supreme God of the universe. When in the future God would bring about eschatological deliverance for Israel, God would also include the gentiles—but not in a way that required gentiles to become Jews. Instead, God would save gentiles *as* gentiles. The nations would stream to Jerusalem and to God's temple, but they would not convert and become Jews.[16] In the meantime, many Jews thought that gentiles were idolatrous and immoral people, but they did not seek to convert them. Other Jews thought gentiles could please the one supreme God by worshiping only this God and living a moral life, free from idolatry, sexual sin, and violence, but without needing

---

14. See Goodman, *Mission and Conversion*, 70–71.
15. Josephus, *Jewish Antiquities* 20.44. Cf. Schwartz, "God, Gentiles, and Jewish Law."
16. For the variety of Jewish thinking about gentiles, see Fredriksen, "Judaism"; Donaldson, *Judaism and the Gentiles*; and Simkovich, *Making of Jewish Universalism*.

to convert to Judaism. Either way, gentiles did not need to become Jews for Israel's God to be gracious and deliver them.[17]

Inasmuch as ancient Jews gave any thought to God's desire or plan to deliver and protect non-Jews from eschatological wrath (and surely many ancient Jews did not have the free time to spend on such abstract questions), they held different positions about how gentiles should relate to Israel's God and to Israel and to Jewish laws. Some thought all non-Jews were excluded from God's saving acts (e.g., the book of Jubilees), others thought God approved of non-Jews who worshiped him and lived ethical lives as gentiles (e.g., later rabbis), while yet others thought God would, at the end of human history, intervene to save non-Jews, again precisely as non-Jews (e.g., the "Animal Apocalypse" in 1 Enoch). And finally, some Jews were convinced that gentiles needed to become Jews to participate in God's deliverance.

Judaism didn't believe anything about the gentiles and deliverance. *Jews*, on the other hand, believed a variety of things about gentiles. These diverging beliefs were at times in conflict and competition with one another. And these differences could result in disagreement between individual Jews and rival groups of Jews. But these variegated convictions all fit within the larger religious tradition that we now refer to as Judaism. When we as modern readers encounter Paul's letters and we see conflict between Paul and others about how exactly gentiles were to relate to Israel's God, to Israel, and to Israel's laws, we are seeing a particular inflection and extension of a much broader conversation that Jews were involved in as they negotiated the ancient Mediterranean world under the conviction that they were God's chosen people, blessed with God's oracles and laws, living in a sea of humanity that was distinct from them.

We can see in Paul's own writings evidence that he held more than one of these positions himself. In his letter to the Galatians, Paul alludes to a time when he was convinced that gentile men needed to adopt circumcision and the Jewish law more broadly (Gal. 5:11). This conviction led him to act much like the Eleazar Josephus mentioned—going

17. See Novak, *Image of the Non-Jew in Judaism.*

out of his way to "proclaim circumcision." But at some point in his life, Paul changed his mind on this approach to gentiles. The next chapter tackles this change in Paul's thinking, but I want to stress that both theological positions on the gentiles and their relationship to Judaism existed prior to and after Paul. And neither position placed Paul outside the spectrum of Judaism.

4

Paul, an End-Time Jew

P aul never wrote an autobiography. Why would he when he expected an imminent end to the current structure of the cosmos? This apocalyptic expectation was central to Paul's thinking. In what many scholars believe to be his earliest surviving letter, Paul responds to followers of the Messiah in the city of Thessalonica who were unsettled by the fact that some of them had died and might, as a result, miss out on God's deliverance. These followers expected the Messiah's return and the dawning of God's kingdom to happen imminently, but as the weeks, months, and even years passed, and as Messiah followers began to die, they understandably became concerned that anyone who had already died had missed out on the promised deliverance. Paul corrects this belief, but not by telling them that it was going to be two thousand years or more before the Messiah returned. He too thought that Jesus was coming shortly—so soon that Jesus would come in the lifetime of many of his first readers:

> For this we say to you by the word of the Lord: We who are alive, who remain until the coming of the Lord, will in no way precede those who have

already died. For the Lord himself, with a summons, with the sound of
the archangel, and with the trumpet of God, will descend from heaven,
and the dead in the Messiah will rise first. Then we who are alive, who
are left, will be caught up in the clouds together with them to meet the
Lord in the air; and so we will be with the Lord forever. (1 Thess. 4:15–17)

Given that the letter was intended to address readers in Thessalonica
who were alive during Paul's lifetime and not people such as ourselves,
who read this letter almost two thousand years later, the *we* Paul mentions here must, in his mind, have included some of his first readers.
Paul expected Jesus to return during the lifetime of some of his readers
(and possibly during his own lifetime). But he was also convinced that
those who had already died had not missed out.

And in a later letter he provides advice to his readers in the city
of Corinth based on his belief that "the time has grown short" (1 Cor.
7:29). Consequently, he instructs readers, "Let even those who have
wives be as those who do not, and those who mourn as those not
mourning, and those who rejoice as those not rejoicing, and those
who buy as those not having, and those who deal with the cosmos as
those not dealing with it" (7:29–31). Believers should live their lives
unencumbered by their present conditions because the "structure
of this cosmos is passing away" (7:31). In this advice, Paul seems to
be participating in Jewish apocalyptic thinking, which encouraged
a certain detachment from the bonds of the current state of affairs
since the end was imminent. For instance, a late first-century Jewish
apocalyptic text known as 4 Ezra contains the following instructions:

Let him that sells be like one who will flee; let him that buys be like one
who will lose; let him that does business be like one who will not make a
profit; and let him that builds a house be like one who will not live in it;
let him that sows be like one who will not reap; so also him that prunes
the vines, like one who will not gather the grapes; them that marry, like
those who will have no children; and them that do not marry, like those
who are widowed. (16.41–44)[1]

1. Translation from Charlesworth, *Old Testament Pseudepigrapha*, 1:558.

Shortly after this advice, Paul claims that the scriptures were written specifically for him and his readers, because upon them "the ends of the ages have come" (1 Cor. 10:11 NRSVue). Paul's letters repeatedly attest to the fact that he was convinced that Israel's God was about to act decisively to defeat sin, death, and Satan, bringing about God's kingdom once and for all (1 Cor. 15). And he envisages this end coming soon: "Look, I will tell you a mystery! We will not all die, but we will all be changed, in a moment, in the twinkling of an eye, at the last trumpet. For the trumpet will sound, and the dead will be raised imperishable, and we will be changed" (1 Cor. 15:51–52 NRSVue). Again, Paul's use of *we* here points to his belief that some of the first readers of this letter were going to live until the Messiah's return and so would not experience death. Such people would need to undergo a bodily transformation from a perishable flesh-and-blood body to an imperishable body fit for the heavenly realm. As Albert Schweitzer stressed over a century ago, "From his first letter to his last Paul's thought is always uniformly dominated by the expectation of the immediate return of Jesus."[2]

With the imminent culmination of human history in sight, Paul did not set out to write a theological treatise akin to Katherine Sonderegger's *Systematic Theology*, or his own autobiography like Augustine's *Confessions*, or a comprehensive vision of the Christian moral life such as Hak Joon Lee's *Christian Ethics*. What Paul did leave behind was a few short literary remains, letters that were perhaps never intended to be read beyond a few small groups of Jesus followers.[3] Scholars debate which of the thirteen letters that bear his name Paul actually wrote and which of them later Christians wrote in his name. We know with certainty that some Christians did write letters, signing Paul's name to them. As far as I know, no one today

---

2. Schweitzer, *Mysticism of Paul the Apostle*, 52.
3. Some scholars have suggested that Paul was responsible for gathering his own letters into a collection (see Trobisch, *Paul's Letter Collection*). If so, Paul would have been doing what his contemporaries, such as Cicero and Pliny, did. Even still, surely Paul could not have anticipated two thousand years of readers all around the world poring over his writings—with some even making a career out of such work and others paying to take courses and buy books devoted to his letters.

believes that Paul wrote 3 Corinthians, even though the letter bears his name and some early Christians, especially in the East, thought it was authentic. And the Muratorian Canon mentions two other letters that claim to be written by Paul—one to the Laodiceans (see Col. 4:16) and one to the Alexandrians, both of which it considers spurious.[4]

The question for readers of Paul's letters is this: Did any spurious letters make it into the New Testament? For historians, this is an open question. On the low end, many scholars believe Paul wrote only seven of the letters that bear his name: Romans, 1 Corinthians, 2 Corinthians, Galatians, Philippians, 1 Thessalonians, and Philemon. On the high end, some scholars think all thirteen letters that bear his name are authentic.[5] And some add Hebrews to Paul's writings even though its author does not claim to be Paul. I do not think Paul wrote the Pastoral Letters (1–2 Timothy, Titus), and I remain uncertain about Ephesians, Colossians, and 2 Thessalonians. Nonetheless, I will cautiously use the evidence of all the letters. Even if Paul wrote all thirteen letters that bear his name, modern readers are left with only a little more than two thousand verses of Paul's thinking, presumably just the tip of the iceberg of Paul's thought and teachings.

How do we reconstruct his thinking, or his theology, from so few writings? Trying to do so is more akin to trying to reconstruct Martin Luther's theology from his *Table Talk* or from seven to thirteen of his sermons than reconstructing his thought from his *Commentary on Galatians* or from the rest of his extensive writings. Paul did not intend to provide his readers with a full account of his Christology or pneumatology or any other topic. And he did not intend to write something systematic. Rather, his literary remains are occasional and rhetorical, intended to provoke the correct thinking and actions from his intended audience despite his absence. And he doesn't provide readers with his spiritual autobiography—though he does tell us a bit

4. The fullest recent treatment of ancient Christian pseudepigrapha—that is, writings composed in another person's name—is Ehrman, *Forgery and Counterforgery*.

5. On some of the problematic assumptions related to authenticity, see White, *Remembering Paul*.

about his life before he became convinced that Jesus is the Messiah and that God raised this crucified Jesus from the dead.

In his two letters to the Galatians and Philippians, Paul provides his readers with a few details about his life prior to encountering Jesus. What do we learn about him? To followers of Jesus in Philippi Paul relates details about his family: first, that he is an Israelite; second, that he comes from the tribe of Benjamin in particular; third, that his parents were born Jews (the Greek says, "a Hebrew out of Hebrews"); and fourth, that his parents circumcised him eight days after he was born (Phil. 3:5). In a list that demonstrates why he should have great confidence in the flesh, the first four items Paul names relate to things that he inherited, not to any achievements Paul himself accomplished. After all, no newborn baby chooses their parents, and no eight-day-old boy ever asks to be circumcised or submits to this rite in any meaningful way. Paul stresses his genealogical descent and his ethnicity. Elsewhere he emphasizes similar aspects of what we would call his identity. To the Corinthians, and in response to competition, Paul claims that he is a Hebrew, an Israelite, and from the seed of Abraham (2 Cor. 11:22). And to the Romans, Paul stresses that he is an Israelite, from the seed of Abraham, and from the tribe of Benjamin (Rom. 11:1). Repeatedly, then, Paul points to his ethnicity, defined most commonly in terms of his genealogical descent—a Hebrew man born to Hebrew parents who is biologically descended from Abraham's seed.[6] Paul defines Jewish identity in what anthropologists call an "essentialist" way—that is, according to the belief that one's ethnicity is a fixed essence or an ontological status that one inherits physically through birth from one's parents, who inherited it from their own parents, all the way back to some primordial point in the past.[7] Paul's ethnic identity is rooted in his genealogical connections, which run through his parents and ancestors back to Benjamin, Jacob, and Isaac, and ultimately back to Abraham and Sarah. In his mind, Paul is a Jew by nature (*physei*), as he puts it in his letter to the Galatians (2:15).

6. Eyl, "'I Myself Am an Israelite.'"
7. For one of the most helpful treatments of essentialist and constructivist conceptions of ethnicity, see Gil-White, "How Thin Is Blood?"

Genealogically Jewish, Paul also mentions that he worked to live in a way that was faithful to his inherited status as an Israelite and Jew. He characterizes himself in superlative terms: With regard to the law, he claims that he is a Pharisee. With regard to righteousness in the law, he claims that he is without blame (Greek: *amemptos*). And with regard to zeal, he points to the fact that he persecuted the *ekklēsia*, the gathering of people following Jesus (Phil. 3:5–6). These last three accomplishments Paul also boasts about in his letter to the Galatians (1:13–14). There he claims that he "advanced in *Ioudaismos*" beyond many of his peers and that he was zealous for the traditions of the elders, a phrase that likely hints again at Paul's upbringing within the tradition of the Pharisees. And, as in Philippians, Paul also acknowledges that he had, at one point in time, persecuted followers of Jesus.

What led to Paul's transformation from someone who persecuted followers of Jesus to one zealous to make as many non-Jewish Jesus followers as possible across a wide geographical region? It was not, as so many popular accounts of Paul suggest, some deep dissatisfaction with his Jewish way of life. Rather, Paul makes it sound like he was quite content and was accomplished in his earlier way of living out Jewish customs and practices, and Israel's God simply interrupted him by revealing God's son Jesus to him.[8] And the point of this interruption? God had authorized Paul to become the Messiah's herald to non-Jews (Gal. 1:15–16). As Krister Stendahl, later the Church of Sweden bishop of Stockholm, argued almost fifty years ago, Paul did not undergo what we would call a "conversion," changing one religion (Judaism) for another (Christianity).[9] Remember, Christianity did not exist in Paul's day. Instead, he found himself believing that his ancestral God, the God of Israel, had called him, a Pharisee who had previously resisted this upstart band who followed some failed and crucified Messiah, to go proclaim a message about the way in which Israel's God, through a resurrected Jewish Messiah, was reclaiming

8. See the account of Kim, *Origins of Paul's Gospel*.
9. Stendahl, "Apostle Paul."

the entire cosmos, non-Jews included, and doing so in fulfillment of Jewish scriptures.

Paul did not abandon Judaism. However, as I mentioned in the previous chapter, this is the impression many translations give in how they deal with the Greek of Galatians 1:13. For instance, the NRSVue translates Paul's words here as "You have heard, no doubt, of my earlier life in Judaism." A better translation would reflect that Paul is speaking about his former manner or way within something he calls *Ioudaismos*, a noun related to the verb *ioudaizein* (to Judaize), which has to do with non-Jews adopting Jewish customs (Gal. 2:14). Jews can't Judaize, but gentiles can. Here Paul claims that formerly he used to promote Jewish practices among gentiles, a claim that he makes more fully in Galatians 5:11, where he states that he used to proclaim circumcision. But even this relatively clear statement contains uncertainty.

To whom did Paul proclaim circumcision? Jews or gentiles? The most reasonable reading of this statement is that he used to proclaim circumcision to non-Jews, since any Jews he spoke to would have been either women, who did not need circumcision, or men, who were already circumcised. It is possible that Paul declared to Jews the abiding validity of circumcision so that they would continue to circumcise their newborn babies, but this would require that enough Jews were giving up the practice of circumcising their sons that Paul had to go around exhorting them to keep at it. It seems more likely that he intends to signify that in the past he taught that gentiles needed to undergo circumcision. This, after all, is the precise thing he seeks to argue against in Galatians.

When, though, did Paul advocate for circumcision? Was it before or after the Messiah was revealed to him? There is no certain answer to this question. It is quite plausible that it took Paul some time after he came to believe that Jesus is the Messiah and had been raised from the dead to arrive at the conclusion that gentiles did not need to and should not undergo circumcision.[10] This latter possibility is strengthened somewhat if we remember, as I argued in the previous chapter,

10. See here D. Campbell, "Galatians 5.11," and Garroway, *Beginning of the Gospel*.

that ancient Jews weren't focused on proselytizing non-Jews. None-theless, I think Paul refers here *primarily* to his actions as a Pharisee before he encountered the risen Messiah. While Jews didn't have mis-sion boards that sent out missionaries to the gentiles, we have some limited evidence that a few Jews did missionize and that some of these people had connections to the Pharisees (Matt. 23:15; also a probable Pharisee named Eleazar in Josephus, *Jewish Antiquities* 20.17–47). So it could make sense that Paul the Pharisee was also involved, however systematically, in proselytizing non-Jews.

Even still, was the issue of whether (male) gentile followers of Jesus needed to undergo circumcision and were the questions about what Paul calls "the works of the law" at the forefront of his mind during the first years after he joined the Jesus movement? Paul tells his read-ers in Galatia that after God revealed the Messiah to him, he went to Arabia. Here he would have been surrounded by Arabians who practiced circumcision in imitation of their ancestor Ishmael, who was circumcised at the age of thirteen (Gen. 17:25). Josephus tells his readers that this was the custom in the first century CE: "The Arabs defer the ceremony [of circumcision] to the thirteenth year, because Ishmael, the founder of their race, born of Abraham's concubine, was circumcised at that age."[11] Consequently, Paul would have been sur-rounded by relatives (however well they got along) of the Jews, since it was commonly believed that Arabians were Abraham's descendants via Ishmael.[12] As Anna Maria Schwemer and Martin Hengel suggest, Paul might have gone to Arabia initially because he believed that Arabi-ans were descendants of Abraham.[13] In Arabia, then, Paul would have been confronted not with foreskinned gentiles but with circumcised Arabian descendants of Abraham. Only once he left Arabia for other gentile territories would the question of whether male gentile believers in Jesus needed to undergo circumcision become an actual issue. This

11. Josephus, *Jewish Antiquities* 1.214.
12. E.g., Jubilees 20.12–13 (trans. VanderKam, *Book of Jubilees*): "Ishmael, his sons, Keturah's sons, and their sons went together and settled from Paran as far as the entrance of Babylon—in all the land toward the east opposite the desert. They mixed with one another and were called Arabs and Ishmaelites." Cf. Josephus, *Jewish Antiquities* 2.32, 213.
13. Hengel and Schwemer, *Paul between Damascus and Antioch*, 118.

controversy would cause Paul considerable frustration, as his letters to Galatia, Philippi, and Rome indicate.

This and the preceding chapter set the contextual stage for what comes next. We are about to wade into the polemically heated climate of Paul's letters, letters that have been interpreted for almost two thousand years to show Paul's break with Judaism and especially the Jewish law. I have argued that Paul did not convert from an established religion called Judaism to a new religion called Christianity. Rather, ancient Jews sought to live out fidelity to their God as they thought best, but they often disagreed with one another on exactly what that looked like and how to make such decisions. And Jews disagreed over something fundamental to Paul's vocation and letters: how to deal with non-Jews. Or better, Jews disagreed over how non-Jews were to relate to Israel, Israel's God, and Israel's law.

5

The Gentile Problem

Paul insistently refers to himself as the *apostolos* of the Messiah. The language of sending (*apostol-*) occurs forty times in the thirteen letters attributed to Paul, almost always referring to Paul. Only three letters ascribed to Paul do not apply the term *apostolos* to Paul: two of them (2 Thessalonians and Titus) may not have been written by Paul, and the other (Philemon) is a letter in which Paul only very lightly stresses his authority. Paul is *the* divinely authorized ambassador for the Messiah. And just as modern ambassadors have circumscribed roles to play, so did Paul. Modern nation-states send out different ambassadors to different countries, seeking to commission the right person, someone who will know how to represent the interests of their own nation within the specific cultural context of the nation to which they are sent. Paul is the Messiah's ambassador not to all humanity but to non-Jews only.

He makes this claim repeatedly in his letter to the Romans: God has called him to be an envoy for the good news (1:1), a proclamation meant to elicit the obedience of loyalty or fidelity of all the gentiles (1:5). He tells the Romans that he desires to visit them so that he can declare the good news there just as he has among the rest of the gentiles, be they Greeks or barbarians (1:13–15).[1] And when he discusses the fact that so many of his fellow Jews do not believe that Jesus is God's Messiah, he mentions again that he is God's envoy to *gentiles* (11:13). Finally, at the close of the body of Romans he claims that he is God's public servant to the gentiles (15:16).

Similarly, to the Galatians Paul avers that God set him apart while he was in his mother's womb and revealed his son to him so that Paul would herald the good news of God's son to the gentiles (1:15–16). And he stresses that God entrusted him with the good news and sent him to gentiles. He contrasts this ethnically specific role to the divinely ordained role of Peter, whom God commissioned as a herald to Jews (2:7–8).

Other early writings of the Jesus movement also emphasize that Paul's ambassadorial role focused on gentiles. Ephesians depicts Paul claiming to be a prisoner on behalf of gentiles because God had commissioned him to make known a mystery and revelation. What was this mystery? That gentiles could become heirs of the promise given to the Messiah (Eph. 3:1–8). Colossians makes very similar assertions about Paul's commission to this mystery and its relation to gentiles (1:24–27). The author of 1 Timothy, writing in Paul's name, depicts Paul as a herald, an envoy, and a teacher of the gentiles (2:7), again connecting him to the mystery of the good news and its relation to gentiles (3:16), while the author of 2 Timothy depicts Paul mentioning God's strength, which enabled him to make the proclamation of the Messiah known to all gentiles (4:17). And finally, the Acts of the Apostles repeatedly depicts Paul as the Messiah's ambassador to the gentiles (14:27; 15:12, 23; 21:19; 22:21) but initially extends this work to

1. On the credentialing nature of the opening verses of Romans, see Jewett, "Romans as an Ambassadorial Letter." Paul's distinction between Greeks and barbarians is how Greeks (and some Romans) divided up humanity. It's roughly equivalent to saying the civilized and the uncivilized or the moral and the immoral. For instance, Plutarch, *On the Fortune of Alexander* 329C–D: the distinguishing mark of the Greek was virtue, while the distinguishing mark of the barbarian was iniquity. Tacitus speaks of the fickle loyalty (*fluxa fide*) of barbarians (*Histories* 3.48) and the absence of "mercy and justice" among them (*Annals* 12.11). Paul then seeks to elicit the obedience of *pistis* (fidelity or trust or loyalty) of gentiles, something that Greeks thought barbarians were incapable of.

the Jews as well (9:15; 26:20). Only as Paul meets with mixed responses among Jews in a particular city does he then turn his focus to non-Jews (13:46–48; 18:6; 28:28).

All of this evidence, both internal and external to Paul's own writings, *requires* us to ask the following questions: Why did Paul primarily seek to proclaim this message about a Jewish Messiah to *gentiles*? Why did he think they needed this message? If Paul could distinguish between good news for the foreskin (Gal. 2:7), a message that targeted non-Jews, and good news for the circumcision, a message that targeted Jews, what made the former distinctive? And why would gentiles be interested in this message? What did they think they could gain from it? After all, rulers and politicians gain or retain power and elicit loyalty from others when they are able to convince their subjects that they rule on behalf of and to the benefit of their subjects. So what benefits did a Jewish Messiah bring to non-Jews? What was the gentile problem or condition that Jesus the resurrected Messiah addressed?

Paul provides us with a relatively full explanation of the gentile condition in Romans, but our modern Bibles hide this fact from us. Consulting the most popular English Bible translations, one can see a common theme. Most of them claim or imply that in Romans 1:18–32 Paul describes the *universal* human condition. A sampling of the added section headings in popular English Bibles shows the following: "God's Wrath Against Sinful Humanity" (NIV), "The Guilt of Humankind" (NRSVue), "Everyone Is Guilty" (CEV), "Unbelief and Its Consequences" (NASB), and "God's Wrath on Unrighteousness" (ESV). But I have discovered two translations (previously unknown to me) that rightly title the section. The CEB labels these verses in this way: "Gentiles Are without Excuse." And the CSB contains the following heading: "The Guilt of the Gentile World." Modern Bible translations disagree with one another because there are no corresponding section titles in the Greek of Paul's letters. These headings are modern additions, added to help readers navigate their thousand-page Bibles. As such, they represent the various interpretations of the committees or individuals that produced these translations. But both the internal evidence of Romans 1 and the external evidence of the earliest readers of Paul's letter to the Romans support the ethnically specific interpretation: Paul here indicts not all of humanity but only the non-Jewish world. To clarify, I am not saying that Paul believed Jews were without sin, were never guilty of breaking the law, or did not need divine forgiveness and grace. But when he wrote Romans 1, he was thinking of and describing a specifically *gentile* condition.[2]

Before looking at some of the details of this indictment, let me address the one slender piece of evidence that has been used to support the belief that Paul intended to indict all humanity: his statement that the people he describes have "exchanged the glory [*hēllaxan tēn doxan*] of the immortal God for images resembling a mortal human or birds or four-footed animals or reptiles" (Rom. 1:23 NRSVue). To those who have ears to hear, Paul's statement might evoke Psalm 106:20 (LXX 105:20), which states, "And they [Israel] exchanged their glory [*hēllaxanto tēn doxan*] for a likeness of a bull calf that eats grass." But Paul does not use the phrase "*their* glory"; instead he speaks of "the glory *of the immortal God*," showing that he is at best riffing here—perhaps using scriptural language but not seeking to cite this text or call it to his readers' attention. The psalm alludes to the tradition of the golden statue of a calf that Israel made in the wilderness (Exod. 32), not to some long-standing and generally idolatrous condition, which is what Paul describes here. His depiction likely draws on the created order (*ktisis kosmou*, Rom. 1:20) of Genesis 1 to indict gentiles for abandoning the immortal creator for mortal creatures—human, bird, four-footed animal, and reptile (cf. these four categories of living beings in Gen. 1:20–24). While there is some shared language, the contexts differ considerably, showing that Paul does not have Israel in mind here.

Paul repeatedly emphasizes the non-Jewish identity of the people on whom divine wrath falls. First, he points to the fact that these people are wicked despite being able to know certain things about God, particularly his eternal power and divine nature, through examination of the created order (Rom. 1:19–20). The people Paul describes

---

2. Young, "Ethnic Ethics."

here have *limited* knowledge of God, knowledge that they derive from the world around them. They appear to lack access to or knowledge of the oracles that God has entrusted to Israel (Rom. 3:2). If they had the Jewish law and scriptures, they would be even more guilty! Since Paul makes no mention of these benefits, it appears that they simply don't have them.

Further, the indictment that these people rejected God and then devolved into idolatry also fits non-Jews (Rom. 1:23). To be sure, Jewish scriptures point to *moments* when Israel committed idolatry, and Paul mentions a few such instances himself (Rom. 11:4; 1 Cor. 10:7–10). Nonetheless, few Jews or non-Jews in the first century CE would have thought that idolatry was a current and widespread Jewish problem. Jews were renowned for their aniconic worship of God, while iconic representation of divine beings was a specifically gentile matter. For instance, in the second-century BCE Letter of Aristeas, one of the Jewish translators of the Septuagint says to the king of Egypt, "And yet, even today, there are many of greater inventiveness and learning than the men of old, who nevertheless would be the first to worship [idols]. Those who have invented these fabrications and myths are usually ranked to be the wisest of the Greeks."[3] Closer to Paul's day, Philo makes a sweeping statement about non-Jewish idolatry and contrasts it to Jewish piety: "When [the gentiles] went wrong in what was the most vital matter of all, it is the literal truth that the error which the rest committed was corrected by the Jewish nation which passed over all created objects because they were created and naturally liable to destruction and chose the service only of the Uncreated and Eternal."[4]

Roman writers from Paul's day make these precise accusations against their own people, claiming that while Roman cultic practices were originally aniconic, they descended into iconic, and therefore inferior, forms of worship. About a century before Paul wrote Romans, Varro bemoans contemporary Roman iconic practices and contrasts

3. Letter of Aristeas 137. Translation from Charlesworth, *Old Testament Pseudepigrapha*, 2:22.
4. Philo, *Special Laws* 2.166.

them unfavorably with the aniconic worship of the Jews.[5] And around
the end of the first century CE, the Roman philosopher Plutarch claims
that within two centuries of the founding of Rome, the Romans had
fallen into iconic worship of the gods.[6] Other non-Jewish writers, both
before and after Paul, show their awareness that Jewish sensibilities
preclude representing their divinity with images.[7] Neither Paul nor
his Roman readers would have understood the accusation of idolatry
to apply to Jews. Idolatry was a distinctly gentile error. And it is this
original idolatry that serves as the wellspring for the immorality that
Paul documents in the remaining verses of Romans 1. For Paul, once
gentiles abandon the living and immortal God for the images of mortal
beings, God hands them over into greater degrees of impure living. In
this, Paul agrees with the Wisdom of Solomon, which, after detailing
at some length the depravity of idolatrous gentiles, concludes, "For
the worship of unnamed idols is the beginning and cause and end of
all evil" (14:27).

Another piece of evidence that Paul focuses exclusively on gentile
sins can be found in his claim that this initial idolatry has led these
people into sexual immorality, particularly homoerotic behavior
(Rom. 1:24–27). Just as idolatry was distinctly gentile, so too, in Jewish thinking, were such sexual activities. For instance, the Letter of
Aristeas distinguishes Jews from non-Jews, claiming that only the latter engage in both homoerotic behavior and incest.[8] And Philo claims,
however accurately, that while non-Jews are sexually profligate from
adolescence, Jews come to marriage as virgins.[9] Philo assumes that
Jewish sexual activity is heteroerotic in nature, not homoerotic, and

---

5. Varro, quoted in Augustine, *City of God* 4.31 (trans. Green).

6. Plutarch, *Life of Numa* 8.8; cf. Plutarch, fragment 158.

7. This awareness of Jewish aniconism is widespread and can be found as early as
the fourth century BCE in the work of historian and philosopher Hecataeus of Abdera,
as reported in the first century BCE by Diodorus of Sicily (*Historical Library* 40.3.1–4);
in the decades immediately prior to Paul's life by the Greek geographer Strabo (*Geography* 16.2.35) and the Roman historian Livy (*Scholia in Lucanum* 2.593); and in the early
second-century CE writings of the Roman historians Tacitus (*Histories* 5.5.4) and Cassius
Dio (*Roman History* 37.17.2).

8. Letter of Aristeas 152. Translation from Charlesworth, *Old Testament Pseudepigrapha*, 2:152.

9. Philo, *On Joseph* 43.

that it always occurs within the bounds of marriage. So too the Sibylline Oracles makes the claim that Jews did not engage in the homoerotic activities for which people groups like the Phoenicians, Egyptians, Latins, and Greeks were known.[10] The nature of the sexual activities of this people (Rom. 1:26–27) was not something Jews thought was a Jewish issue: it was a distinctively gentile practice.[11]

Beyond the evidence of the letter, early external evidence suggests that this is precisely how ancient readers would have understood the passage. Contrary to most modern interpreters, early Christian interpreters fully recognized that the list of behaviors in Romans 1:18–32 describes gentiles and only gentiles. All early interpreters of Romans 1:18–32 understood the passage to be Paul's invective against gentiles. Here I will provide only a sampling of evidence of how early *gentile* readers understood Romans 1:18–32.[12]

In the late second century CE, Tatian addresses the men of Greece, citing Romans 1:20 as the reason why he and other Christians refuse to follow the Greeks in the worship of creation.[13] Likewise, Irenaeus avers that those who "worship and serve the creature rather than the creator" (Rom. 1:25) are gentiles.[14] Clement of Alexandria also notes that in Romans 1:18–32 Paul makes accusations against the Greeks.[15] Similarly, on the basis of Paul's claim that though they knew God through his creation, they did not honor him as God (1:19–20), Origen concludes that Paul describes gentiles alone: "For there is a difference between knowing God and knowing God's will. God could be known even by the Gentiles 'from the creation of the world through the things that have been made, and through his external power and deity.' His will, however, is not known except from the law and the prophets."[16] In a similar way, Origen understands Paul's statement that these people

10. Sibylline Oracles 3.596–600.
11. On homosexuality in a Roman context, see the important work of C. Williams, *Roman Homosexuality*.
12. Gaca, "Paul's Uncommon Declaration"; see Thiessen, *Paul and the Gentile Problem*, 47–52, for my fuller argument.
13. Tatian, *Oration against the Greeks* 4.2.
14. Irenaeus, *Against Heresies* 4.33.1.
15. Clement of Alexandria, *Exhortation to the Greeks* 8.
16. Origen, *Commentary on Romans* 2.7.1 (trans. Scheck); cf. *Against Celsus* 3.47.

did not honor God (Rom. 1:21) to refer to gentiles: "The Apostle seems to condemn the Gentiles because, though they knew God by natural understanding, they did not honor him as God."[17] Again, Origen understands Romans 1:22–24 to refer only to gentiles: "Therefore he accused certain Greeks, i.e., the Gentiles, of being under sin."[18]

In the fourth century, Athanasius composed a work with two volumes, *Against the Pagans* and *On the Incarnation*, in which he depicts the vices of the non-Jewish Greco-Roman world. Such people, he argues, "glorified creation instead of the creator," a reference to Romans 1:25.[19] He cites Romans 1:21–24 as evidence of the idolatrous practices of the gentile world.[20] And, quoting Romans 1:26–27, he argues that, as a result of worshiping idols, the gentile world descended into sexual immorality, their women giving themselves over to cultic prostitution, their men preferring the sexually passive and receptive role that he believed befitted women.[21]

Another of Paul's earliest commentators, Pelagius, notes that Paul had only gentiles in mind in Romans 1:18: "He begins [to address] the case [of the Gentiles, and he says that the wrath of God is revealed through the Gospel, or else through the testimony of nature]."[22] A prologue to Paul's letters most likely composed by Rufinus of Syria in the late fourth century CE claims that Paul wrote Romans 1 to remind his readers "of their prior vices as gentiles." This example is of particular significance in that it understands Romans 1 to be about gentiles and assumes that Paul intended to address the entirety of the letter only to gentile readers. Similarly, in his *Homilies on Romans*, John Chrysostom repeatedly claims that Paul directs the accusations of Romans 1:18–32 against Greeks (i.e., gentiles; cf. especially homily 3). In homily 5 Chrysostom links Romans 1:28 to Paul's negative comments about

---

17. Origen, *Commentary on Romans* 2.7.6 (trans. Scheck).
18. Origen, *Commentary on Romans* 3.2.3 (trans. Scheck); cf. *Against Celsus* 4.30.
19. Athanasius, *Against the Pagans* 8.29–30 (trans. Thomson); cf. 47.18–19; *On the Incarnation* 11.26–27.
20. Athanasius, *Against the Pagans* 19.11–17.
21. Athanasius, *Against the Pagans* 26.1–11; cf. *On the Incarnation* 5.28–34.
22. Pelagius, *Commentary on Romans* 1.18 (trans. de Bruyn, *Pelagius' Commentary*); material within brackets is lacking from some manuscripts.

gentiles in 1 Thessalonians 4:5, concluding that "here too he shows that it was to them [the gentiles] the sins belonged."[23] Theodoret of Cyrus claims that at Romans 1:18 Paul begins to accuse all non-Jews of "fearlessly breaking the law placed in nature by the creator," arguing that it is only at 2:10 that he "intends now to introduce the accusation against Jews."[24] Likewise, Ambrosiaster argues that Paul describes gentiles in Romans 1:24–28.[25] Finally, Augustine too believes that Paul intended Romans 1:21–23 to describe gentiles, who "knew [the Creator] but did not give thanks and, claiming to be wise, actually became fools and fell into idolatry."[26] And even though Paul does not explicitly state whose impiety incurs the wrath of God in Romans 1:18, Augustine links this impiety to gentiles alone.[27]

This whirlwind tour provides only a fraction of what the earliest interpreters of Paul had to say about Romans 1:18–32. Most important for our purposes, all of these interpreters were themselves *non-Jewish* readers of Romans. So, while we have no immediate access to how Paul's first readers/auditors in Rome understood Romans 1:18–32, patristic evidence, being written by early gentile readers, is our next best thing. Our earliest extant interpreters of Paul and commentators on his letter to the Romans agree that Romans 1:18–32 addresses the gentile world, not all of humanity, and this despite their varying degrees of animosity toward Jews. I would suggest that this is precisely how Paul's first gentile readers in Rome would have understood the passage.

But the strongest external piece of evidence that Paul intended to depict only gentiles in these verses actually comes from the letter to the Ephesians. In this letter, the author—either Paul or one of his earliest followers—*explicitly* depicts the degraded state of gentiles who do not follow the Messiah: "You must no longer walk as the gentiles walk in the futility of their minds. They are darkened in their understanding, estranged from the life of God because of the ignorance that

---

23. John Chrysostom, *Homilies on Acts and Romans*, NPNF[1] 11:359.
24. Theodoret of Cyrus, *Commentary on Romans* 1:17 and 2:10 (trans. Hill).
25. Ambrosiaster, *Commentary on Romans* 1:24–28 (trans. Bray).
26. Augustine, *Propositions from the Epistle to the Romans* 3.2 (trans. Fredriksen Landes).
27. Augustine, *Propositions from the Epistle to the Romans* 3.5.

is in them on account of the hardness of their heart. Having become unfeeling, they have given themselves over in licentiousness to the work of every impurity in greed" (4:17–19).

The language of this passage, which explicitly names the gentiles, has parallels to the language Paul applies to unnamed people in Romans 1:18–32. Like Paul in Romans, who claims that these people "became futile [*emataiōthēsan*] in their thinking" (Rom. 1:21), Ephesians portrays gentiles walking in the futility (*en mataiotēti*) of their minds (Eph. 4:17). Paul also claims that "their senseless heart has been darkened [*eskotisthē*]" (Rom. 1:21), while Ephesians depicts gentiles as having darkened understanding (*eskotōmenoi*) (Eph. 4:18). And Paul states that God handed over these people (*paredōken autous*), in the desires of their hearts, to impurity (*eis akatharsian*) (Rom. 1:24) and that, consequently, they were filled with all sorts of vices, including greed or lust (*pleonexia*) (Rom. 1:29). Similarly, Ephesians claims that gentiles gave themselves over (*heautous paredōkan*) to every impurity (*eis ergasian akatharsias*) and did so in greed or lust (*pleonexia*) (Eph. 4:19). If Paul wrote Ephesians, then he repeats much of the same language he uses in Romans 1 to explicitly describe the degraded moral condition of non-Jews. If, on the other hand, Ephesians was written by an early disciple of Paul, then that reader understood the language Paul uses in Romans 1:18–32 as language particularly fitting for the gentile world. Either way, it provides strong evidence that in Romans 1:18–32 Paul intends to portray the gentile world and the gentile world only.

Jews often nuanced this negative depiction of the gentile world, recognizing that not all gentiles fit the role of the idolatrous and vice-ridden pagan. But Paul's letters do not do this. The rhetoric Paul repeatedly employs suggests that all gentiles are trapped in idolatrous lives that have resulted in sinful, destructive behavior.[28] In his earliest letter, a letter to gentiles in Thessalonica, Paul calls his readers to distance themselves from their former way of life, assuming that it was

28. One could also point to Paul's speech in Athens at the Areopagus that Luke details in Acts 17. There Luke depicts Paul undone by the fact that the city is filled with idols, evidence of non-Jewish (im)piety, even as he uses concepts from Greek philosophy to call them to the one supreme God.

grossly immoral: "For this is the will of God, your sanctification: that you abstain from sexual immorality; that each one of you know how to control your own body in holiness and honor, not with lustful passion, like the gentiles who do not know God" (1 Thess. 4:3–5 NRSVue).

If you were a gentile who was being told repeatedly, explicitly and implicitly, that your heritage, your customs, and your forms of piety were all the negative results of abandoning the one true God, you might very well ask yourself what you needed to do in order to be saved.[29] Many gentiles who heard this message likely rejected it as an inaccurate and unfair depiction of the gentile condition, but if they accepted it, they might naturally have found themselves wanting to be anything but a gentile. It's into this Jewish understanding of the gentile problem that Paul interjects his message about Jesus the Messiah. But who is this Jesus, and how does he solve the gentile problem?

---

29. While acknowledging that Rom. 1:18–32 depicts gentiles, Douglas Campbell (*Deliverance of God*, 516–47) has suggested that these verses represent the position of Paul's interlocutor and not Paul's own thinking. The evidence of Eph. 4:17–19 and 1 Thess. 4:3–5 shows that this is indeed Paul's position. Paul had no problem with ethnic stereotyping, a common practice in the ancient world, whatever we might think about it. Cf. Isaac, *Invention of Racism*.

6

Jesus the Messiah

Especially since the Protestant Reformation, Paul's message has often been summarized as being about justification by faith or about salvation by grace and not through works. I do not dispute that these are elements of Paul's thinking, but at the center of Paul's message lies not a proposition but a person: Jesus. Considering only the seven undisputed letters, Paul mentions the name Jesus almost 150 times (it's over 200 if we consider the evidence of all thirteen letters). And he uses the word *christos* (anointed) 269 times in those seven letters (it's over 300 if we consider the evidence of the thirteen letters). To put this into perspective, Paul mentions grace (*charis*) 66 times, justice/righteousness language (*dikai-*) 95 times, and trust/loyalty language (*pist-*) 142 times. Paul writes of Jesus over and over, but what does he say about him? If we want to learn about the details of Jesus's life, the letters tell us surprisingly little.

To the Thessalonians, Paul says only that Jesus died (Paul doesn't even mention Jesus's crucifixion), that God raised him from the dead, and that now he resides in heaven, from where he will soon return

(1 Thess. 1:10; 4:14; 5:23).[1] To the Galatians, Paul says this about Jesus: "When the fullness of time had come, God sent his son, born of a woman, born under the law" (Gal. 4:4 NRSVue). Paul's language stresses both Jesus's humanity (born of a woman) and his Jewishness (born under the law). But the claim also appears to imply that God's son preexisted his birth: God *sent* his son (cf. Rom. 8:3).[2] In this letter, too, Paul notes Jesus's death, adding that it happened via crucifixion, which readers would have identified as a Roman form of execution (Gal. 3:1, 13; 6:14).

Confirmation that Paul believed God's son preexisted his birth can be found in his letter to the Philippians. There he tells his readers that Jesus had at one point been in the form (*morphē*) of God but had emptied himself, "taking the form [*morphē*] of a slave, being born in the likeness [*homoiōma*] of humans" (Phil. 2:6–7). Paul's language here evokes the story of God's creation of humanity in Genesis 1:26–27, which describes humans as God's image (*eikōn*) and likeness (*homoiōma*). But whereas the first humans ate forbidden fruit in the hope of becoming like gods (*hōs theoi*, Gen. 3:5; cf. 3:22), Jesus, being already in God's form, traded this elevated status for the lowly likeness of enslaved humanity.[3] This ignoble existence culminated in Jesus's death, an odious death by crucifixion (Phil. 2:8). But God exalted Jesus above all names to the heavens, from where he will one day come (3:20) and be recognized as Lord (*kyrios*) (2:10–11) by all beings in heaven, on earth, and under the earth.

In the letter to the Corinthians, unlike in any other letter, Paul quotes words that he believed Jesus spoke to his disciples on the night

1. He might also say that *some* of Jesus's fellow Jews were responsible for his death (1 Thess. 2:15), but some scholars think that a later scribe added vv. 13–16 to 1 Thessalonians. Regardless of who wrote these verses, the bald description of seemingly all Jews as those "who killed both the Lord Jesus and the prophets" (so the NRSVue and many other translations) is due to translation mispunctuation—wrongly inserting a comma that has no business being there. Instead, the phrase "who killed" applies only to certain Jews. See the important article of Gilliard, "Problem of the Antisemitic Comma."

2. If one thinks that Paul also wrote Colossians, then the hymn of Col. 1:15–20 would provide the strongest evidence for Jesus's preexistence before coming in the flesh, an existence that dates to creation itself. On this hymn, see van Kooten, *Cosmic Christology*.

3. Much has been written on these verses, but the most compelling reading is that of Fletcher-Louis, "'Manner Equal with God.'"

when he broke bread and shared wine with his followers (1 Cor. 11:23–26).[4] He also stresses Jesus's death by crucifixion (1 Cor. 1:17–18, 23; 2:2, 8; cf. 2 Cor. 13:4) and notes that Jesus was buried and raised on the third day, appearing a number of times to over five hundred people, including to Paul himself (1 Cor. 15:4–8).[5]

And to the Romans, Paul emphasizes that Jesus is related to Israel's paradigmatic king, David. In his opening words to believers in the city of Rome, Paul stresses that, with regard to the flesh, Jesus comes from the seed of David (Rom. 1:3). This language highlights not only Jesus's fleshly humanity but also his ethnicity and tribal affiliation (cf. 9:5): he is from the tribe of Judah and related to King David himself. Repeatedly in the letter Paul mentions that Jesus died but that God raised him from the dead (e.g., 1:4; 4:24; 5:6, 8; 6:10; 10:9; 14:9). Paul puts it pithily in Romans 8:34: Jesus the Messiah died, was raised, and is currently at God's right hand, where he intervenes for believers. And in Romans 15, near the end of the body of his letter, Paul quotes the following words from the prophet Isaiah:

> The root of Jesse will come,
> the one who rises to rule the gentiles;
> upon him the gentiles will hope. (Rom. 15:12, quoting Isa. 11:10)

As Seyoon Kim has pointed out, Romans 1 and 15 form "an inclusio with the reference to Jesus' Davidic Messiahship."[6] It is no wonder, then, that a later writer claims that Paul's message is about "Jesus the Messiah, raised from the dead, from the seed of David" (2 Tim. 2:8). But the inclusio formed by Romans 1 and 15 is more detailed than this. It is also a message for the nations, the gentiles (Rom. 1:5–6, 13–15, which quotes Ps. 18:49 [LXX 17:50]).[7] Further, not only do both passages connect the Davidic Messiah to the gentiles, but they also connect the gentiles to obedience: in Romans 1:5 the "obedience of

---

4. It is possible, but far from certain, that Paul also alludes to a teaching of Jesus in 1 Cor. 7:10–11.
5. See Allison, *Resurrection of Jesus*.
6. Kim, "Paul as an Eschatological Herald," 10.
7. Cf. Deut. 32:43; Ps. 117:1 (LXX 116:1); Isa. 11:10.

faith,"[8] and in 15:18 obedience in word and deed. The message that the Messiah's herald brings should be submitted to or obeyed (Rom. 10:16; cf. 2 Thess. 1:8), something that Paul's readers in Rome have done (Rom. 16:19; 2 Cor. 7:15; 10:5; cf. Eph. 6:5). Even in his lengthy greetings that end the letter, Paul again speaks about the need for gentiles to respond with the obedience of faith (Rom. 16:26). It seems that Paul's vision of gentile obedience to Israel's Messiah is indebted to one of Israel's psalms, which depicts the Davidic Anointed saying to Israel's God:

> You appointed me head of the gentiles;
> a people whom I had not known was enslaved to me.
> As soon as it heard, it obeyed me. (Ps. 18:43–44 [LXX
>   17:44–45])

Paul explicitly quoted this verse in Romans 15, so it is obvious he knew it. When he speaks of the gentiles and obedience, then, it appears that he has this passage in mind.[9] Now, through Paul's proclamation, gentiles are coming to obey God's Anointed, the Messiah, in fulfillment of Psalm 18 (LXX 17).

The Messiah's Kingdom

Not all Messiahs were kings, but Paul's Messiah was. Consequently, Paul's Messiah had a kingdom. While the Jesus of the Synoptic Gospels talks about the kingdom of God or the kingdom of the heavens (the latter only in Matthew),[10] it is less commonly noted that Paul too speaks

---

8. This connection between faith and obedience complicates standard theological oppositions of faith to works. As Teresa Morgan (*Roman Faith and Christian Faith*, 282–83) puts it, "*Pistis* . . . is often associated with obedience and the language of service, and 'the obedience of *pistis*' is best read as a genitive of apposition, referring to Paul's sense that the *pistis* into which he brings gentiles is, like his own, a relationship of slavish obedience to Christ."

9. Novenson (*Christ among the Messiahs*, 142) notes that Isa. 11:14, which Paul also quotes in Rom. 15, likewise refers to the Davidic Messiah, the gentiles, and obedience (specifically of the sons of Ammon).

10. See Pennington, *Heaven and Earth*.

about this kingdom.[11] For Paul, all humanity belongs to one of two dominions. Prior to the Messiah's coronation, death and sin reigned as king (Rom. 5:14, 17, 21). Now the Messiah has inaugurated a new kingdom, one in which justice and life rule (5:17, 21). This kingdom of life has displaced and is displacing a kingdom ruled by the hostile powers of sin and death. As Paul, or an early disciple of Paul, puts it, "[God] has rescued us from the power of darkness and transferred us into the kingdom of his beloved son" (Col. 1:13 NRSVue). Repeatedly, Paul emphasizes that participation in this kingdom requires living according to its rules. This kingdom is not about food and drink but about justice, peace, and joy (Rom. 14:17). It is a kingdom of power, not mere talk (1 Cor. 4:20). Those who continue to live unjustly will not inherit God's kingdom (1 Cor. 6:9–10; Gal. 5:21; cf. Eph. 5:5). In his undisputed letter to Thessalonica, Paul exhorts believers to live a life worthy of the God who calls them into his kingdom (1 Thess. 2:12; cf. 2 Thess. 1:5).[12] Believers strive for this kingdom, even as they do not experience its fullness at the present moment, because the Messiah has not yet destroyed all opposition to himself and his rule. That day will come, though, and then believers will undergo a great transformation in order to inherit it (1 Cor. 15:24, 50).

More than anything, Paul's thinking about Jesus revolves around his messianic identity. As mentioned at the start of this chapter, in the undisputed letters, the name Jesus appears almost 150 times, only 34 of which do not immediately connect that name to the title *christos*. In most of these instances Paul identifies Jesus as *kyrios*, "Lord."[13] And of the 269 occurrences of the word *christos* in Paul's seven undisputed letters, over half (159) occur alone. Some have argued that *christos* in Paul had already come to function as an empty name. For instance, James D. G. Dunn confidently asserts, "As all commentators recognize,

---

11. The Acts of the Apostles also depicts Paul proclaiming the coming kingdom of God: Acts 14:22; 19:8; 28:23, 31. The only other reference to God's kingdom in Acts relates to Philip, so Luke connects declarations about the arrival of God's kingdom to Paul most strongly.

12. Both letters to Timothy also emphasize this kingdom (1 Tim. 6:15; 2 Tim. 4:1, 18).

13. There are only eleven exceptions: Rom. 3:26; one occurrence in 1 Cor. 12:3 (although here Paul speaks in the voice of someone cursing Jesus); five occurrences in 2 Cor. 4:10–11, 14; and one occurrence each in Gal. 6:17; Phil. 2:10; 1 Thess. 1:10; 4:14.

'Christ' had already become a proper name in Paul's writing, having already lost most if not all of its titular force."[14] But Matthew Novenson has shown that for Paul it retained its royal honorific function. Jewish messianism, in other words, was central to Paul's thinking, Paul's message, and Paul's understanding of who Jesus is.[15]

Paul's proclamation was a message of good news about one particular person: Jesus. Paul was convinced that this Jesus who had been crucified on a Roman cross was actually God's Messiah, his Anointed. Some of his letters imply that Jesus existed as God's son even before he was born of a woman and took on flesh—a heavenly being of some sort. We might wish that Paul were more specific here, but he isn't. For this reason, scholars debate whether Paul identified Jesus with Israel's God[16] or whether he thought Jesus was initially some lower deity, like an angelic being, who only in the wake of his death and resurrection was exalted over all other deities and angels.[17]

Paul does not take time to reflect on Jesus's preincarnate status but focuses on the fact that Jesus descends from a place of divinity to a place of lowly humanity, taking up flesh and blood. And then he is virtually silent about Jesus's life, though it is possible that Paul alludes to Jesus's teaching at one or two points in his letters. The most probable place that this occurs is in his letter to believers in Corinth: "To the married I give this command—not I but the Lord—that the wife should not separate from her husband (but if she does separate, let her remain unmarried or else be reconciled to her husband) and that the husband should not divorce his wife" (1 Cor. 7:10–11 NRSVue). This command, which Paul attributes to Jesus ("the Lord"), appears

14. Dunn, *New Perspective on Paul*, 352.
15. See Novenson's *Christ among the Messiahs* and *Grammar of Messianism*. On the centrality of messianism to the entire New Testament, see Jipp, *Messianic Theology*.
16. Some believe that Paul equated the Messiah with God in Rom. 9:5, but the Greek here is too ambiguous to provide any answer. Either Paul claims that the Messiah is God or, after mentioning the many blessings of Israel (including the fact that the Messiah comes from Israel), Paul breaks out into praise: "God, who is over all, be blessed forever, Amen!" I think the latter more likely.
17. Classic arguments for Paul's "high" Christology include Bauckham, *Jesus and the God of Israel*, and Hurtado, *One God, One Lord*. See now the excellent collection of essays on this topic in Novenson, *Monotheism and Christology*, especially the essay of Paula Fredriksen.

to be connected to Jesus's prohibition against divorce, which we find later recorded in the Gospels (Mark 10:11; Matt. 5:31; 19:7; Luke 16:18).

Paul's thinking about Jesus, though, is focused not on what deeds he did or on what things he said but on his death, resurrection, and ascension. And the only words he attributes to Jesus (1 Cor. 11:23–26) are those that relate to the cultic meal Jesus established to evoke the memory of his death. Not only did Jesus take on human form, but he also lived a life of obedience to God that resulted in his death on a Roman cross. Why Rome crucified Jesus, Paul does not make known (or does not care to know himself), but he claims that the rulers of this age would not have crucified Jesus had they understood God's plans (1 Cor. 2:8). As scandalous as it was to people, Paul stresses Jesus's crucifixion—publicly depicting Jesus as crucified to the Galatians (3:1) and claiming to boast in nothing but the cross of the Messiah (6:14).[18] And to those in Corinth, Paul states that he proclaims a crucified Messiah, knowing nothing among them but the Messiah crucified, even though he is aware that such a message is a stumbling block to Jews and pure foolishness to gentiles (1 Cor. 1:23; 2:2). A crucified Messiah is utterly scandalous (Gal. 5:11) in the eyes of the world, but Paul believes that this odious death results in benefits for the ungodly and sinners (Rom. 5:6, 8). Jesus died for "our sins" (1 Cor. 15:3). And Jesus died and lived again so that he might be Lord of both the dead and the living (Rom. 14:9).

Although many readers of Paul (and the New Testament more generally) focus on Jesus's death as the locus of God's saving acts, Paul's focus is never solely, and arguably not even centrally, on Jesus's death. His death might be necessary, but it is insufficient. If Jesus had not been raised from the dead, then Paul thinks his good news would be vacuous, and putting one's trust in Paul, his message, or his Messiah would be entirely pointless (1 Cor. 15:13–14). So while Paul teaches that the Messiah died for "our sins" (1 Cor. 15:3), he also claims that people would still remain in those sins if Israel's God had not raised Jesus from

18. Hengel, *Crucifixion in the Ancient World*, 20–21: "The utter offensiveness of the 'instrument for the execution of Jesus' is still to be found in the preaching of Paul." See now the encyclopedic evidence of Cook, *Crucifixion in the Mediterranean World*.

the dead (1 Cor. 15:17). And while Jesus was handed over to death for trespasses, only his resurrection justifies sinners (Rom. 4:25).[19] And it is not believing that Jesus died for one's sins that saves a person but believing that God has raised Jesus from the dead (Rom. 10:9).

When Paul introduces himself and his message to believers in Rome, most of whom do not know him personally, he does not mention Jesus's death, only his resurrection (Rom. 1:3; cf. Gal. 1:1).[20] And while he reflects on the significance of Jesus's death for the moral life in Romans 6, the point or purpose is that the Messiah was raised from the dead by God's glory (6:4). Being raised from the dead, the Messiah is no longer subject to death's rule (6:9).

Jesus's resurrection resulted in his ascension and exaltation to heaven at God's right hand, where he perpetually intercedes for believers (Rom. 8:34; 10:6; cf. Eph. 1:20; 4:8–10; Col. 3:1). Paul tells us that God has given Jesus a name above all other names and that all beings—those in heaven, those on earth, and those under the earth—will submit and confess that Jesus is Lord (*kyrios*) (Phil. 2:9–11). The Messiah who did not view equality with God as something to seize violently and who suffered obediently to the point of crucifixion, then, attains equality with God, being also named *kyrios*, Lord, the same word that Jews frequently used to translate the Hebrew divine name, Yhwh.[21] Finally, the Messiah will one day soon return from heaven to rescue believers from the coming wrath, raising both the living and the dead to eternal life.

Abraham's Seed, the Messiah

Paul's messianism is thoroughgoing and central to his self-understanding as a herald of the good news and to his understanding of what Israel's God is now doing to redeem the world, gentiles included. But

19. On the connection between resurrection and justification, see D. Campbell, *Deliverance of God*, 747.

20. Kirk, *Unlocking Romans*. On the centrality of resurrection to Galatians, see Boakye, *Death and Life*.

21. A. Meyer, *Naming God in Early Judaism*.

Paul situates this messianism within a larger context of God's deal-
ings with Israel's primordial ancestor, Abraham. In his letter to the
Galatians, Paul makes a claim that has frustrated or flummoxed many
of his readers (3:16). He states that God made a series of promises to
both Abraham and Abraham's seed (Greek: *sperma*). (Similar claims
can be found in Rom. 4.) He then makes what looks very much like a
specious grammatical argument, noting that the Jewish scriptures say
"seed" (*sperma*), not "seeds" (*spermata*). On the basis of the singular
form of the noun, Paul claims that Abraham's seed refers not to all of
Abraham's offspring but to one particular individual. Who? The Messiah. For Paul, Jesus is Abraham's seed. Consequently, the promises
that God gave to Abraham centuries earlier are now coming to fulfillment in relation to Jesus the Messiah.

Now it's true that the Greek of Genesis refers to Abraham's *sperma*,
a grammatically singular noun (the Hebrew *zera* is also singular), but
just as with the English word *seed*, *sperma* frequently functions as a
collective singular.[22] We all know that if someone says they scattered
seed onto a field, this does not mean they threw only a single seed
onto the field. Out of the almost 250 times that the Septuagint uses the
word *sperma*, only five times does it use the grammatically plural form
spermata.[23] Instead, it frequently uses the singular form, but it refers to
numerous individual seeds, such as in the creation narrative of Genesis
1, where God creates seed-bearing plants (1:11–12). So Paul's claim that
the singular form must mean one singular offspring is shaky.

Numerous interpreters have tried to explain how Paul came to this
conclusion. Most rightly point to the use of seed language in God's
words to King David: "I will raise up your seed [*sperma*] after you,
who shall come out of your innards, and I will establish his kingdom"
(2 Sam. 7:12). But one relatively common word (*sperma*) is an admittedly slim link between the Abraham narrative and King David's seed.
Strengthening this connection, Novenson points to the fact that both

---

22. We don't know for certain which passage from the Abraham narrative Paul has in
mind since the phrase "to your seed" (always *sperma* and never *spermata*) occurs several
times: Gen. 12:7; 13:15; 15:18; 17:8; 22:18.

23. Lev. 26:16; 1 Sam. 8:15; Ps. 125:6; Isa. 61:11; 4 Macc. 18:1.

2 Samuel 7:12 and Genesis 17:7 use the language of *seed* in connection with related verbs: 2 Samuel uses *anistēmi*, while Genesis 17 uses *histēmi* as well as the phrase "after you" (*meta sou*).[24] I have elsewhere sought to connect 2 Samuel 7:12 to yet another passage in the Abraham narrative, Genesis 15:4, since in the Hebrew both passages refer to seed that comes forth from David's and Abraham's *innards*.[25]

Whatever one thinks of his interpretive moves here, Paul's point is that the promises that God made to Abraham were also promises he made to the Messiah: promises of a blessing (Gen. 12:2–3; Gal. 3:14), promises of territory (Gen. 12:7; 13:15; 17:8; Rom. 4:13),[26] promises of a covenant (Gen. 17:7; Gal. 3:17), promises of a kingdom (Gen. 17:6, 16; cf. Eph. 5:5; Col. 1:13), promises of, in short, inheritance (Gen. 15:4; Gal. 3:18). Anyone who wants to inherit all these promises must somehow become connected to both Abraham and the Messiah. What, then, are gentiles to do? After all, they are not genealogically descended from Abraham. Can they somehow forge a new connection to Abraham and the Messiah to access these promises? If so, how?

Conclusion

Whatever else Paul has to say, the core of his message is about Jesus, who he has come to believe is the Jewish Messiah, who preexisted his incarnation, who was sent down to earth by Israel's God to take on human flesh, who lived in obedience to God even though it resulted in his crucifixion, and whom God raised from the dead, declared son of God, and seated at his right hand. This evidence points to a clear pattern of movement: from up to down and up again. As Douglas Campbell puts it, "One story of Christ is involved here but it contains two distinctive internal movements or trajectories; one from 'sending,' through suffering, to death; and the other from death,

---

24. Novenson, *Christ among the Messiahs*, 141–42.
25. See Thiessen, *Paul and the Gentile Problem*, 124–27.
26. On how land expands to the entire cosmos in some later Jewish thinking, including Paul's, see McCaulley, *Sharing in the Son's Inheritance*.

through resurrection, to heavenly glorification (cf. Phil. 2:5–11)."[27] It is this Messiah who has inherited the promises God made long ago to Abraham and who will return triumphantly to conquer all anti-God forces, destroying death (1 Cor. 15:54–56) and Satan (Rom. 16:20) and fully establishing the kingdom of God (Rom. 14:17; 1 Cor. 4:20; 6:9; 15:24, 50; Gal. 5:21; 1 Thess. 2:12), a kingdom that is celestial in nature (Phil. 3:20). That is the great news that Paul is appointed to share with gentiles, but the question that dogged him and others was how these gentiles could access these promises. The next two chapters examine this pressing issue, first by looking at one solution, which was promoted by people Paul deemed his opponents, and then by looking at the solution Paul himself offers. While they disagreed on the way to do so, both were convinced that it was essential that gentiles become genealogically connected to Abraham and Abraham's seed, the Messiah. Why? Because this is the only way that gentiles can become fellow heirs and fellow sharers in the promise (Eph. 3:6).

27. D. Campbell, "Story of Jesus," 106–7.

7

The Gentile Problem and Cosmetic Surgery

I am a Mennonite whose ancestors migrated to Ukraine at the invitation of Catherine the Great in the late eighteenth century. When my German-speaking ancestors subsequently migrated to North America, they divided their world into two categories: Mennonites and *the English*. I grew up in a town that had large Italian, Portuguese, and Lebanese communities. They were all *the English* to some of my older Mennonite relatives. (These communities would have been shocked and insulted to hear this.) Mennonites used that catchall category to describe non-Mennonites because when they communicated with others, they spoke English, as opposed to the German dialect Mennonites initially spoke.[1] Of course, the category flattened all non-Mennonites into one thing, ignoring that many people spoke English only as a second or third language and were not English in the sense of being in some way connected to England. And while the

---

1. One can see the continued use of *the English* in the title of a recent dystopian novel about the Amish in Pennsylvania: D. Williams, *When the English Fall*.

title had a generally neutral meaning on its surface, it often implied something negative about people's worldliness. For example, I understood very well what my elderly relative was implying when she met my now spouse and asked her, "Oh, is that an *English* name?"

That impulse to divide the world into two groups, an insider group (one's community) and an outsider group (everyone else), was very common in the ancient world. And negative caricatures of other ethnic groups abounded in the ancient Mediterranean world.[2] The Roman philosopher Plutarch, for instance, claimed that Greeks were virtuous and distinct from vicious barbarians (that is, everyone else).[3] And many ancient Jews viewed non-Jews negatively.

Gentiles who frequented Jewish settings likely heard negative depictions of the gentile world from time to time. When that happened, they might have become defensive or uncomfortable. Think of Paul's unrelentingly negative depiction of gentiles in Romans 1: gentiles are idolatrous and sexually immoral people who face God's wrath. How would such a generalization strike gentiles who heard it? And for that matter, would it have bothered gentiles that Paul rarely took the time to distinguish between different types of non-Jews, lumping all of them into the catchall and rather derogatory category of *the gentiles*?[4] No non-Jew would have done this.[5] The difference between a Galatian and a Corinthian was the difference between Korean and Chinese, or Italian and Nigerian. Non-Jews did not divide the world into Jews and gentiles. That was a Jewish way of viewing the world.

Despite this, many gentiles wanted to be loyal followers of a Jew named Jesus, believing him to be a Jewish Messiah who would deliver them. They had perhaps been attending the local Jewish synagogue, rubbing shoulders with Jews who welcomed them into their gatherings even as they distinguished between Jews and non-Jews. Gentiles

2. See the impressive evidence collected in Kennedy, Roy, and Goldman, *Race and Ethnicity*, as well as the discussion of Isaac, *Invention of Racism*.

3. Plutarch, *On the Fortune of Alexander* 329C–D.

4. For a thorough discussion of the phrase *the gentiles*, see Ophir and Rosen-Zvi, *Goy*, and the helpful corrective essay of Hayes, "Complicated Goy."

5. Only in the wake of Paul and the rise of Christianity did Christians begin to own the title *gentiles*. See here Donaldson, *Gentile Christian Identity*.

regularly heard Jewish sacred texts read and discussed. And they heard about the God of the Jews and the Jewish belief that their God, despite all appearances to the contrary, ruled over the Roman Empire and was the supreme God over the entire cosmos. For many reasons, gentiles may have felt comfortable within these communities of Jews and found their way of life attractive.

Gentile Attraction to Jewish Practices

While Peter Schäfer has documented evidence of ancient anti-Judaism, his book tells only part of the ancient story. Most gentiles despised Jewish customs and practices, but others were attracted to them.[6] Jewish piety resonated with certain "pagan" cultural values, which at times valorized aniconism. Many Jews and non-Jews believed that there were many gods but only one supreme God.[7] And this supreme God was far above all else, utterly different from the created realm. For this reason, Jews generally refused to depict their god in paintings or images. For instance, one of their sacred texts frequently condemned the making of idols: "You shall not make for yourself a carved image, whether in the likeness of anything that is in heaven above, or that is on the earth below, or that is in the water beneath the earth. You shall neither bow down to them nor worship them" (Deut. 5:8–9). Writing in the first century CE, the Jewish philosopher Philo of Alexandria likewise condemned idolatry: "Let no one, then, who has a soul worship a soulless thing, for it is utterly preposterous that the works of nature should turn aside to do service to what human hands have wrought."[8] Jews were known for their refusal to depict their god, as the Roman historian Tacitus notes: "The first Roman to subdue the Jews and set foot in their temple by right of conquest was Gnaeus Pompey: thereafter it was a matter of common knowledge that there were no representations of the gods within, but that the place was empty and the secret shrine contained nothing."[9]

---

6. Schäfer, *Judeophobia*, and Cohen, "Respect for Judaism by Gentiles."
7. Fredriksen, "Philo, Herod, Paul."
8. Philo, *On the Decalogue* 76.
9. Tacitus, *Histories* 5.9.

But Jews weren't the only ones to decry visible depictions of the supreme God. Writing shortly after Paul, the Roman philosopher Plutarch claims that Pythagoras believed that the supreme divinity was invisible and beyond the senses and so could not be depicted in images. Plutarch goes on to argue that Numa, the second king of Rome and a paragon of religious piety, "forbade the Romans to revere an image of God which had the form of man or beast."[10] Indeed, the first two centuries of Rome's existence, he avers, were free from the making of statues and paintings to use in worshiping the supreme deity. Elsewhere, in a fragmentary text, Plutarch makes the sweeping generalization that in antiquity humanity "did not choose to hack a stone into a hard, awkward, lifeless image of a god."[11]

Plutarch probably did not invent these traditions about both Pythagoras and Numa, and so they must have been relatively well known to many people in the Roman Empire. And we see in Seneca the Younger, a contemporary of Paul, a similar denigration of images depicting the divine. In his now lost work *On Superstition*, Seneca pens the following criticism of common human piety: "To beings who are sacred, immortal, and inviolable they consecrate images of the cheapest inert material. They give them the shapes of humans or beasts or fish; some, in fact, make them double creatures of both sexes combined or unlike bodies united. They are called divinities, but if they were successfully brought to life and encountered, they would be regarded as monsters."[12] A good number of gentiles, then, might have found Jewish aniconism to be a superior form of devotion to the supreme God.

What is more, some gentiles looked at the Jewish way of life and found in it a model of virtuous living.[13] Dietary and sexual restrictions may have appealed to some who sought to control their passions and desires, overcoming the weakness of the flesh to live virtuously. We have evidence that some Jews promoted the Jewish law as a gift from God that was meant to order people's desires properly. For instance,

---

10. Plutarch, *Numa* 8.7–8.
11. Plutarch, fragment 158.
12. Seneca the Younger, *On Superstition*, quoted in Augustine, *City of God* 6.10.
13. See Aune, "Mastery of the Passions."

Philo asserts that when gentiles adopt the Jewish law, they "become at once temperate, self-mastered, modest, gentle, kind, humane, serious, righteous, high-minded, truth-lovers, superior to wealth and pleasure, just as conversely the rebels from the holy laws are seen to be incontinent, shameless, unjust, frivolous, petty-minded, quarrelsome, friends of falsehood and perjury, who have sold their freedom for dainties and strong liquor and delicacies and the enjoyment of another's beauty, thus ministering to the delights of the belly and the organs below it— delights which end in the gravest injuries to body and soul."[14]

At about the same time that Philo argues that the Jewish law takes formerly vice-ridden gentiles and transforms them into virtuous people, the author of 4 Maccabees makes similar claims. Even the (seemingly) most random laws serve to inculcate one in virtue. For instance, numerous law collections in the Pentateuch prohibit the charging of interest (Exod. 22:25; Lev. 25:36–37; Deut. 23:19–20). Further, the book of Deuteronomy requires that debts be canceled every seven years (Deut. 15:1–18) and prohibits people from stripping all their crops for a profit: "When you reap your harvest in your field and forget a sheaf in the field, do not go back to get it; leave it for the immigrant, the orphan, and the widow, so that Yhwh your God may bless you in all your doings. When you beat your olive trees, do not strip what is left; it will be for the immigrant, the orphan, and the widow. When you harvest the grapes of your vineyard, do not pick what is left; leave it for the immigrant, the orphan, and the widow" (Deut. 24:19–21).

All of this legislation focuses on the need to care for the marginalized within the land of Israel: those who need loans or have debts or have no land from which to provide for themselves. The author of 4 Maccabees, though, suggests that these laws provide care not only for the marginalized but also for the people privileged enough to own property: "As soon as one adopts a way of life in accordance with the law, even though a lover of money, one is forced to act contrary to

14. Philo, *On the Virtues* 182, slightly modified from the Loeb Classical Library translation.

natural ways and to lend without interest to the needy and to cancel
the debt when the seventh year arrives. If one is greedy, one is ruled
by the law through reason so that one neither gleans the harvest nor
gathers the last grapes from the vineyard" (2:8–9).

Another example: Leviticus 11 and Deuteronomy 14 command Israel to abstain from eating the meat of certain animals. These texts
provide no specific rationale as to why some animals are edible and
others are not, but the command is to do this because Israel should be
holy as God is holy (Lev. 11:44–45; Deut. 14:21). The author of 4 Maccabees, though, relates keeping the food laws to restraining the bodily
appetites through reason (4 Macc. 1:31–35).[15] The Letter of Aristeas,
which was written much earlier, connects dietary laws to justice and
just relations between humans.[16] What Philo, the author of 4 Maccabees, and no doubt some other Jews believed was that God had given
the law to them and that this law was a powerful gift that enabled them
to overcome sin and vice to live a just and righteous life that pleased
God. If the law, a gift from God, was divinely imbued with this power,
surely any gentiles who wanted to transcend their sinful states should
turn to Israel's God and Israel's law. Here was a distinctively Jewish
solution to the problem of what many people in the Greco-Roman
world were trying to address.[17]

Abraham and Gentile Circumcision

Any gentile who chose to inhabit Jewish spaces and Jewish communities might also have felt a certain amount of pressure or discomfort
when existing in these places, worshiping the Jewish God, and reading
Jewish scriptures while still identifying and living as a gentile. What
would a gentile man think, for instance, when Genesis 17, a text that

---

15. Some ancient people considered pork to be the richest of meats, and so one could
argue that avoiding the most luxurious of foods was a way of training oneself to curb
desire. See Galen, *Method of Medicine* 7.482K. For a convincing account of the underlying
moral vision behind the dietary codes, see Weiss, "Bloodshed and the Ethics."

16. Letter of Aristeas 169.

17. See Nussbaum, *Therapy of Desire*; Fitzgerald, *Passions and Moral Progress*; and Max
Lee, *Moral Transformation*.

describes God's covenant of circumcision with Abraham and his children, was read or discussed in communal settings? Surely one question would be how the rite of circumcision related to him and his family. Was this covenant available to gentiles, and if so, would he be required to get circumcised? If he wanted to be part of Abraham's family, was the rite of circumcision the way to join it?

One Jewish text, the book of Judith, suggests that at least some Jews thought this to be the case. In this fictional work, one righteous gentile named Achior the Ammonite observes God's miraculous deliverance of Israel from the military might of the Assyrians. "Because Achior saw all that the God of Israel had done," the author states, "he was greatly loyal to God, circumcised the flesh of his foreskin, and was added to the house of Israel to this day" (Jdt. 14:10). What is striking about this terse remark is that it draws on the Abraham narrative of Genesis, connecting Achior both to Abraham's loyalty to God (Gen. 15:5) and to Abraham's circumcision (Gen. 17:24). It's a great story, but that's all it is—fiction, not history.

But we see something quite close to this narrative situation with regard to an actual historical person in the writings of Josephus. He tells the story of a gentile named Izates, who was king of Adiabene.[18] At some point during his reign, Izates became acquainted with a Jewish merchant named Ananias. This Ananias had already taught gentile women in the city of Charax-Spasini (located in modern-day southern Iraq) to worship God according to the ancestral way of the Jews. Presumably this worship included esteeming the Jewish God as the supreme God, not depicting this God in images, and also adhering to a certain ethical code, what Terence Donaldson has called ethical monotheism.[19] Through these women, Izates too began to worship God in this way. Such worship, though, led him to the decision that he should undergo the rite of circumcision and "be steadfastly Jewish."[20] But both Ananias and Izates's mother temporarily convinced him that he did not need to get circumcised in order to please God.

---

18. Josephus, *Jewish Antiquities* 20.34–48.
19. Donaldson, *Judaism and the Gentiles*, 662–69.
20. Josephus, *Jewish Antiquities* 20.38. The Greek states: *einai bebaiōs Ioudaios*.

Subsequently, another Jewish teacher, this one named Eleazar (likely a Pharisee), arrived and changed Izates's mind. When Eleazar saw Izates reading the law of Moses, he scolded him in the following way: "In your ignorance, O king, you are guilty of the greatest offence against the law and thereby against God. For you ought not merely to *read* the law but also, and even more, to *do* what is commanded in it. How long will you continue to be uncircumcised? If you have not yet read the law concerning this matter, read it now, so that you may know what an impiety it is that you commit."[21] Convinced by the logic of Eleazar's accusation against him, Izates immediately called for a surgeon and had himself circumcised.

Put yourself in Izates's sandals or, for that matter, in the sandals of a first-century gentile follower of Jesus. You have begun to think about the world in Jewish terms. You worship the one supreme God of the world and identify this God with the God of the Jews—the God of Abraham, Isaac, and Jacob. You have regularly been reading Jewish scriptures (or have been hearing them read regularly). What do you do when you read or hear a text like Genesis 17? Surely one of the most natural responses, if you are a gentile *man*, is to wonder whether you too should undergo circumcision. Should you just read the text, or should you perform the rite that the text says functions as a sign of God's covenant with Abraham? After all, Abraham was himself from the nations (a Chaldean—a gentile!), not a Jew. And he trusted in God and then subsequently underwent the rite of circumcision. Perhaps you should as well.

As reasonable as this reading and response to Genesis 17 might be, Paul dismisses it. But Paul does not claim that gentiles merely do not *need* to undergo circumcision, as scholars often suggest. Instead, he positively *prohibits* gentile men from undergoing circumcision. As he tells his Galatian readers, "Listen! I, Paul, am telling you that if you let yourselves be circumcised, the Messiah will be of no benefit to you" (Gal. 5:2).[22] The reason he gives for this pronouncement is that gentile followers of the Messiah who undergo circumcision are seeking

21. Josephus, *Jewish Antiquities* 20.44–45.
22. See here Collman, *Apostle to the Foreskin*.

to be justified by their observance of the Jewish law. In so doing, he tells them, you "have cut yourselves off from the Messiah; you have fallen away from grace" (5:4). I will unpack these comments later, but here I want to discuss Paul's rebuttal of his opponents' reading of Genesis 17.

Anticircumcision Texts in Paul

For two thousand years Christians have almost universally understood Paul to be dismissing circumcision as a mere physical rite that has no value—this is the common understanding of the anti-legalistic, anti-ethnocentric, and apocalyptic readings of Paul. And such an understanding implies or explicitly promotes the idea that Paul rejects Genesis 17 (and Lev. 12) because he has abandoned the Jewish law (and Judaism). Consequently, gentile Messiah followers should not practice the rite, and Jewish Messiah followers should stop circumcising their sons. For evidence of this interpretation, they point to texts like Philippians 3:2, where Paul refers to his opponents, who are promoting circumcision, as "the mutilation" (*katatomē*). The implication seems to be that Paul thinks circumcision is nothing other than a rite that disfigures one's body, using language from Leviticus that condemns the mutilation of the flesh (Lev. 21:5). Or they point to Romans, where Paul supposedly claims that physical circumcision is nothing and that real circumcision is the metaphorical or spiritual circumcision of the heart. Such a statement seems clear from the NRSV translation of Romans 2:28–29:

> For a person is not a Jew who is one outwardly, nor is true circumcision something external and physical. Rather, a person is a Jew who is one inwardly, and real circumcision is a matter of the heart—it is spiritual and not literal. Such a person receives praise not from others but from God.

But this rendering of the Greek, despite how commonly variations of it occur both in translations and in commentaries, is a considerable overinterpretation of Paul's actual words. A rough translation of the Greek here is as follows:

> For it is not the visible Jew, nor is it the visible in-flesh circumcision, but the hidden Jew, and the circumcision of the heart by the *pneuma*, not the letter, whose praise is from God, not from a human.

Contrary to virtually every English translation of these verses, not once does Paul use a word that means something like *real* or *true* here. The point is not that one form of circumcision is real and the other is false, but that God requires more than being a visible Jew or being physically circumcised. Being a Jew or being genitally circumcised does not in itself automatically qualify one for God's praise. Rather, a person with a circumcised heart merits God's praise.

If this sounds like a radical thought, one that undermines or abandons the Jewish law, it is not. Rather, it was a widespread Jewish belief that God desired Jews to be circumcised in the heart, not just in the flesh. One can see this in Deuteronomy, where being circumcised in the heart means to be compliant and obedient (Deut. 10:16; cf. Lev. 26:41) and results in love toward God (Deut. 30:6). For ancient Jews, this was not an either-or matter. Faithful Jews (well, male ones) were physically circumcised *and* circumcised in their hearts. The prophet Jeremiah seems to make precisely the same point Paul does in Romans 2, condemning Israel along with a bunch of other circumcised nations. Though Israel is rightly circumcised in the flesh (unlike other circumcised nations who are *wrongly* circumcised in the flesh), Israel is uncircumcised in their hearts (Jer. 9:25–26).

What is more, Paul also explicitly states the opposite of what Christian readers frequently claim he says. Immediately after these verses, which suggest God's praise is for those who are circumcised of heart, he ensures his readers that his claims are no denunciation of physical circumcision. His literary questioner asks, "[If this is so], what then is the value of being a Jew or of circumcision?" (Rom. 3:1). Perhaps, one might conclude, physical circumcision has no value. Paul rejects this conclusion as false: "Much in every way!" (Rom. 3:2).

Unfortunately, many of Paul's interpreters have not taken him at his word here. If there is indeed value to circumcision, why does Paul refer to his circumcision-encouraging opponents as the *mutilation* (Phil. 3:2)? The answer can be found in remembering Paul's intended audience in Philippi: a group of gentile Messiah followers. Any gentile who undergoes circumcision is, in Paul's mind, *not* undergoing covenantal circumcision; rather, they are undergoing a rite that mutilates the flesh and brings them no salvific benefit. Paul's identification of circumcision as mutilation is *not* a universal statement about the value of circumcision, only a condemnation of gentile circumcision efforts: for Jews, circumcision is of value (Rom. 3:1–2); for gentiles, circumcision is a detrimental bodily mutilation. It is a ritual that fails to bring any benefit and instead causes harm.[23]

We see similar logic at play in Romans 4, where Paul discusses Abraham at some length. Paul begins by asking what Abraham discovered with regard to the flesh (*sarx*)—in other words, circumcision.[24] That is, if Paul's gentile readers are seeking to emulate Abraham, perhaps it would be of value to determine what Abraham discovered about the circumcision of the flesh. Paul provides a brief reading of the Abraham narrative, suggesting that the episodes are chronologically ordered and that this chronology matters for his gentile readers. In summary, Paul argues that since Genesis 15 occurs before Genesis 17, Abraham was reckoned as righteous prior to his circumcision. In this way, Abraham's life demonstrates that God forgives the sins of the foreskinned just as he does the sins of the circumcised. God's blessing of forgiveness is available, then, both to circumcised and to foreskinned, both to Jews and to gentiles.

But this raises an important question. If God had already blessed Abraham and forgiven him, why did Abraham need to undergo circumcision in Genesis 17? Paul's answer is quite surprising. He claims

---

23. See Neutel, "Circumcision Gone Wrong," and Smit, *Felix Culpa*.

24. This is how the early Christian interpreter known as Ambrosiaster understood the text in his *Commentary on Romans* 4:1. So too Pelagius, *Commentary on Romans* 4:1. In contrast, the NRSVue translation "our ancestor according to the flesh" is, simply put, impossible. Given that Paul addresses non-Jewish readers, he could not have described Abraham as their ancestor by flesh. By *pistis* and *pneuma*, yes. By *sarx*, never.

that God called Abraham to undergo circumcision *so that* he would
then become the father to all who trust, both the foreskinned gentile and the circumcised Jew. It sounds like Paul believes that had
Abraham trusted God's promises in Genesis 15 but then not undergone circumcision, he could only be the father of gentile Messiah
followers—since both he and they were foreskinned. Consequently, he
needed to undergo circumcision so that he could also be the father of
Jewish Messiah followers. This is a startling claim. But Paul's point is
that Abraham's circumcision had value in that it became a means for
God first to create a distinct people of Israel and then to demonstrate
that circumcised Jewish Messiah followers were also included in God's
deliverance.

Abraham's Sons and Seed

In Galatians, Paul focuses less on using Abraham as an example and
more on how one becomes a son and seed of Abraham. Consequently,
he looks to Abraham's first two sons (Abraham also had six often-
forgotten sons with Keturah; Gen. 25:1–4). In Galatians 4:21–31, Paul
talks about one type of sonship that results in slavery and a second type
of sonship that results in freedom.[25] These verses make up one of the
most poorly understood passages in Paul's letters, primarily because
of an erroneous interpretation of what Paul means when he refers to
the Abraham narrative as an allegory (Gal. 4:24).

Virtually every interpreter has concluded that Paul claims that *he*
is providing an allegorical interpretation of the purportedly historical
book of Genesis. That is, most think Paul is allegorizing here and does
so in a way that undermines the original intention of Genesis, which
included the requirement for all males to undergo circumcision to
be part of Abraham's covenantal seed. To put it bluntly, this reading

---

25. While I wholeheartedly support inclusivity and equality in modern contexts, I
resist translating *huioi* (sons) and *adelphoi* (brothers) in a way that hides the gendered
nature of Paul's language. Yes, Paul uses this language of both men and women, but the
point is that both men and women are *sons* and *brothers* precisely because they participate
in the Messiah, who is God's son. Again, let Paul be weird.

implies *either* that Paul dramatically misunderstood the meaning of Genesis *or* that he simply did not care about its meaning and was trying to deceive or confuse his gentile readers so that they would do what he wanted. While historians should have no qualms about entertaining either possibility, I think there is a good reason to suggest that both possibilities are wrong.

Paul does not say that *he* is providing an allegorical interpretation of Genesis. Instead, he claims that the Abraham narrative itself *is* an allegory. The difference is significant. It is the difference between treating a historical work on the civil rights movement as an allegory about Jesus and treating John Bunyan's *The Pilgrim's Progress* or George Orwell's *Animal Farm* as an allegory. In the former case, the allegorizing work is placed on the shoulders of the reader; in the other, the allegorizing was intended by the author and so readers should decipher this original allegorical intention correctly. Paul claims that the Abraham narrative was written as an allegory. In other words, the original intention of the Abraham narrative was to provide a story about Abraham and his sons that was allegorical in meaning. And in Galatians 4:21–31 Paul seeks to show his readers what this original meaning was and how it applies to their lives now. This was the meaning that *allēgoria* commonly had in Paul's day, as one can see in the works of Greco-Roman writers such as Heraclitus and Tryphon as well as Jewish writers such as Josephus and Philo. Allegory was a literary device used by authors, *not* an external hermeneutical strategy deployed by later readers on a nonallegorical text.[26] The trick, then, was to learn to recognize which texts were originally allegorical and then to figure out how to read them accurately.

If Paul thinks the story of Abraham has an allegorical intention, what does he think it teaches him and his readers? It's quite simple and straightforward. The gentile men of Galatia are considering circumcision. And some of them may already have undergone the rite in the

---

26. Tryphon, *On Tropes* 1.1; Heraclitus, *Homeric Problems* 1.1, 3; 5.13; 22.1; 29.4; 41.12; 75.12. Cf. the translation by Russell and Konstan (*Heraclitus*, xiii–xv), which provides evidence that this meaning of *allegoria* goes back to the sixth century BCE. Philo claims that "all or most of the law-book is an allegory" (*On Joseph* 28), while Josephus says that at times Moses speaks about God allegorically (*Jewish Antiquities* 1.24).

hope of becoming Abrahamic sons and seed. Paul thinks this is not only a dead end but also devastatingly detrimental. And he believes scripture itself shows this to be the case. He reminds his readers, therefore, that Abraham had more than one son and that not all of them made it into the covenant. Indeed, only one of them did and only one of them was reckoned the seed of Abraham.

Paul then briefly summarizes the details in the Abraham narrative that matter for his scriptural case against gentile circumcision. He starts by asking whether those who wish to be under the law actually hear or obey the law (Gal. 4:21). What are they not hearing? First, that Abraham had two sons, with two very different origins and two very different outcomes. One son was born to one mother, an enslaved woman (Hagar), while the other son was born to another mother, a free woman (Sarah). The son born to the enslaved woman was born according to the flesh, Paul says. This description fits Ishmael well, who was born as a result of the actions of Sarah and Abraham and through natural, fleshly means: traditional sexual intercourse (Gen. 16:1–3). The narrator of Genesis 16 emphasizes fleshly, human efforts: Sarah did not bear, Sarah had a slave, Sarah said, Abraham listened, Sarah took Hagar, Sarah gave Hagar, Abraham went into Hagar, and Hagar conceived. Not once does the author mention God's actions apart from Sarah's telling confession that God had prevented her from having children (16:2). The author's language evokes the story of the transgression of Adam and Eve in the garden:

> Eve *took* the fruit and *gave* it *to her husband* (3:6)
> Sarah *took* Hagar and *gave* her *to her husband* (16:3)

> Adam *listened to the voice of his wife* (3:17)
> Abraham *listened to the voice of* [*his wife*] Sarah (16:2)

In contrast, Isaac was born through the promise, a promise that God made to two elderly people who could not expect to have children naturally, both because of age and because of Sarah's barrenness (Gen. 11:30; 16:2; 18:11). Here the emphasis lies in God's acting: "The LORD dealt with Sarah as he had said, and the LORD did for Sarah as he had promised" (21:1 NRSVue). The narrator of Genesis 21 stresses divine action to the point that one might wonder what role (if any) Abraham played in Isaac's conception. Two sons from two mothers, born in two very different ways. Having argued that Ishmael was birthed according to *flesh,* Paul has now forged a link between Ishmael's birth and the efforts of gentiles in Galatia to be born as Abrahamic sons via the rite of circumcision, a practice Paul refers to with the word "flesh" (*sarx*) (Gal. 3:3; 6:12–13). If one tries to become a son of Abraham through the fleshly rite of circumcision, beware, because Abraham's original fleshly son, Ishmael, failed to inherit.

A quick glance at the Abraham narrative suggests Paul might have more in mind, even if he does not spell it out. Abraham's two sons both underwent the rite of circumcision: Ishmael in Genesis 17:23–27 and Isaac in Genesis 21:4. By the logic of Paul's opponents, *both* Ishmael and Isaac should therefore be Abrahamic sons and Abrahamic seed. They should both be members of God's covenant with Abraham and therefore heirs to God's promises to Abraham. But this is decidedly not the case. Genesis 17 itself makes this crystal clear. God gives the covenant of circumcision to Abraham and to his seed (17:9–14) at a time when Abraham already has a son named Ishmael. And yet God immediately tells Abraham that his wife, Sarah, will have a son (17:15). Abraham appears to realize what this promise implies: Ishmael is not the promised son. Consequently, Abraham asks God to recognize Ishmael (17:18). God responds by saying that he will indeed bless Ishmael, but he sandwiches this blessing with an emphatic declaration that Ishmael will still not be the Abrahamic son with whom God will make an eternal covenant. The covenant son will come through Sarah and will be named Isaac (17:19–21). The text merits quotation:

> And Abraham said to God, "O that Ishmael might live in your sight!"
> God said, "No, but your wife Sarah shall bear you a son, and you shall name him Isaac. I will establish my covenant with him as an everlasting covenant for his seed after him.

"As for Ishmael, I have heard you; I will bless him and make him fruitful and exceedingly numerous; he shall be the father of twelve princes,
and I will make him a great nation.

"But my covenant I will establish with Isaac, whom Sarah shall bear
to you at this season next year." (Gen. 17:18–21 NRSVue alt.)

What this text makes apparent is that being circumcised does not guar-
antee that one is part of God's covenant with Abraham and his seed.
Abraham circumcised his slaves, and this was even required (Gen.
17:12), but these circumcised enslaved men did not thereby become
heirs to this covenant. Father Abraham did indeed have many sons
(and slaves), but only one inherited from Abraham: "Abraham gave
all he had to Isaac" (Gen. 25:5).

One could therefore conclude, and at least one ancient author did
(the author of the book of Jubilees), that a significant difference between Ishmael and Isaac is that only Isaac undergoes the rite of circumcision correctly.[27] After all, Genesis 17:12 and 17:14 (and also Lev.
12:3) require circumcision to take place on the eighth day after birth.
Genesis stresses that Ishmael was circumcised when he was thirteen
(17:25) and that Isaac alone underwent circumcision eight days after
being born (21:4).

From this difference in the timing of their respective circumci-
sions, one could conclude that anyone who undergoes circumcision
later than the eighth day imitates Ishmael and not Isaac. And since
Ishmael was the son of an enslaved woman, this made him and those
who imitated him enslaved people as well. Enslaved people are not
inheriting sons, though. And the Abraham narrative makes this ex-
plicit. Even though God sent the pregnant Hagar back to Abraham's
household and promised to bless her future son (16:7–10), Ishmael did
not become a permanent fixture in Abraham's household. And since
Ishmael did not inherit from Abraham, neither do those who imitate
his circumcision. Even worse, the Abraham narrative describes Ishmael's expulsion from Abraham's house, not his incorporation into it.

27. On Jubilees' treatment of Gen. 17, see Thiessen, *Contesting Conversion*, 67–86.

When Sarah sees Ishmael playing with Isaac, she becomes incensed, demanding of Abraham, "Cast out this enslaved woman with her son; for the son of this enslaved woman shall not inherit along with my son Isaac" (Gen. 21:10). Paul ends his treatment of the Abraham narrative by quoting this very verse (Gal. 4:30). In effect, Paul's reading of Genesis is the following:

> You gentile men want to keep the law, but you haven't read it carefully enough.
>
> You want to be Abraham's sons through circumcision.
>
> But Abraham had *two* circumcised sons: Ishmael (a slave) and Isaac (an heir).
>
> By undergoing adult circumcision, you imitate Ishmael, not Isaac.
>
> Consequently, you will share in Ishmael's fate.
>
> You, like Ishmael, will not inherit.
>
> Instead, you will be cast out of Abraham's house altogether.
>
> Only those who are like Isaac, born according to the *pneuma* and promise, will inherit.

Conclusion

Paul's anticircumcision rhetoric needs to be situated within the actual historical context that occasioned his letters. He is the Jewish Messiah's ambassador to the gentiles, bringing them a message about deliverance. Some of those who have come to trust this Messiah, though, have become confused by the Jewish scriptures that mention the rite of circumcision and other things that Paul may not have mentioned at all. Some of them have, like King Izates, become convinced that they need to undergo circumcision now. In Galatians and Romans in particular, although it lurks in 1 Corinthians and Philippians as well, Paul addresses this possibility, showing from scripture that gentile circumcision is not the same thing as covenantal circumcision. It does not address the gentile problem, and it does not make gentiles into inheriting sons—the seed—of Abraham. Gentile circumcision is nothing more than a cosmetic effort to look like Abraham, but it is one that results only in a superficial, fleshly connection, something too tenuous to be of eschatological, and therefore lasting, value.

8

Pneumatic Gene Therapy

N. T. Wright has famously (or infamously) said that Paul's message stressed "grace, not race."[1] Such a claim implies that Judaism, in contrast, stressed race and not grace. And this is precisely what Wright and James Dunn have argued in claiming that Paul sought to undermine Jewish ethnocentrism. While such arguments fit well with important contemporary concerns around racism and nationalism, I do not think they adequately describe Paul's thinking. As I will argue in this chapter, Paul's writings demonstrate his abiding commitment to ancient ethnic reasoning. Gentiles *need* to become connected to Abraham so that they can inherit God's promises to him and his seed. Paul argues against gentile circumcision not because he is trying to break down ethnic boundaries but because he does not think that circumcision has the power to bridge the genealogical gap between Abraham and the gentiles. For Paul, only the divine power of the *pneuma* (often translated into English as "Spirit") can truly connect gentiles and Abraham. Gentiles, in short, need to

1. Wright, *Climax of the Covenant*, 194, 247.

undergo pneumatic gene therapy in order to inherit the many things God promised to Abraham.

Imagine a first-century gentile. And imagine that this particular gentile has come to believe that a Jewish man named Paul is the envoy of the supreme God of the universe, who also happens to be the God of the Jews. And imagine that this person has become convinced that Paul's rather strange message about an obscure man named Jesus is true. A Jewish man who lived most of his life in the backwater of Galilee is actually Israel's long-awaited Messiah. But despite being the Messiah, Jesus was put to death on a Roman cross. The Roman Empire had crucified many people over the years, and such nobodies were quickly forgotten by all but their families and friends. So a first-century gentile might wonder, Why are people all around the Mediterranean still hearing about Jesus? And why is a small group of Jews telling people that this Jesus is actually their long-awaited Messiah? Why are they declaring that he is God's son? Why is this man named Paul traveling across the Roman Empire telling non-Jews about a Jewish kingly figure, claiming that God has raised this crucified Jesus from the dead? Why would any gentile become convinced by this outlandish message? But if this gentile does believe it, how can they get in on the kingdom of this Messiah?

If, as I argued in the previous chapter, Paul teaches that gentiles cannot become Jews, what options remain? Paul argues that circumcision and adoption of the Jewish law in its entirety will not work for gentiles because Israel's God never intended for non-Jews to undergo circumcision and adoption of the Jewish law.[2] Paul mocks the attempt to become a Jew in this way as little more than an unnecessary and unsightly cosmetic surgery: mutilation, in fact (Phil. 3:2). If a gentile man gets circumcised, he might call himself a Jew (Rom. 2:17) and might even look like a Jew (Rom. 2:28), but he remains nothing but a gentile. Paul thinks this simply won't cut it (sorry for the pun).[3] Circumcision might fool some people, but a circumcised gentile has not addressed

---

2. Eisenbaum, *Paul Was Not a Christian*, 62–63.
3. I'm not actually sorry.

the underlying condition: he has dealt only with the flesh, not the *pneuma*. Cosmetic surgery does not connect a person to Abraham, and so it does not connect that person to God's promises. A foreskinned Abraham had those promises (Rom. 4:10). Conversely, a circumcised Ishmael was not a beneficiary of those very same promises.

Perhaps, one might conclude, it is unnecessary for gentiles to become related to Abraham. Maybe gentiles can be saved as gentiles and just relate to Israel as sympathetic gentiles in the past frequently had. After all, Paul expects gentiles to turn from their dead idols to the living God, abandoning the worship of all gods but the God of Israel (e.g., 1 Cor. 5:11; 6:9; 12:2; 2 Cor. 6:6; 1 Thess. 1:9). Or perhaps gentiles just need to become (ancient) monotheists who adopt a certain moral standard that Jews expect of God-pleasing, righteous gentiles: some variation of the laws that many Jews thought God gave to Noah and all his descendants as a moral baseline.[4] But at least two of Paul's letters complicate such a suggestion. While three of his letters mention Abraham, Romans and Galatians speak about Abraham and Abraham's seed at some length (Rom. 4 and Gal. 3–4). Abraham is the father of all who believe, and those who trust in the Messiah are Abraham's seed (Rom. 4:11, 13; Gal. 3:6, 29). These passages show that Paul believes that gentiles do indeed need to become related to Abraham in order to inherit what God promised. But if circumcision and law are unable to make gentiles into seed of Abraham, what can?

Paul offers a solution, one that later interpreters have often misunderstood. For instance, some readers of Paul have argued that he minimizes the importance and relevance of being related to Abraham by shifting the conversation to being related to God.[5] Who needs to be a son or seed of Abraham when one can be a son of God? But in both Romans 4 and Galatians 3 Paul sets out to show how one becomes a seed of Abraham. Galatians 3:29 provides the clearest distillation of Paul's thinking on this point: "If you are [part] of the Messiah [*ei hymeis Christou*], then you are the seed [*sperma*] of Abraham." For gentiles

4. Novak, *Image of the Non-Jew in Judaism*.
5. Martyn, *Galatians*, 374.

to become Abraham's seed, they only need to belong to the Messiah. One does this by being immersed *into* and being clothed *in* the Messiah. Paul uses the language of containment—entering into (*eis*) and becoming wrapped by or clothed in (*enduō*) the Messiah (Gal. 3:27). Such statements encourage us to think in very spatial categories. The Messiah is a location or a container or a sphere into which gentiles must enter in order to be related to Abraham.[6]

The language of immersion or baptism into the Messiah connects this event to the reception of the *pneuma*, something Paul has already discussed at the beginning of his argument about descent from Abraham in Galatians 3:1–7. There, Paul stresses that Galatian gentile followers of the Messiah had received the *pneuma* not through any works but through the hearing of faith. By receiving with faith the good news that Paul proclaimed, the gentiles became recipients of this powerful *pneuma* (3:1–5). Paul goes on to compare this gentile faith to Abraham's faith in Genesis 15:6, concluding that those who are born out of faith are Abraham's sons (Gal. 3:6).[7] The logic, then, of Galatians 3:1–7 is that through faith one receives the *pneuma* (cf. 3:14). Simultaneously, the one born out of faith becomes a son of Abraham.

But how is this the case? Is Paul just pulling this idea out of a hat? Or is he spiritualizing away descent from Abraham? Does one become a child of Abraham merely by acting or, in this case, thinking like him? Christians for centuries have generally concluded the latter: copying Abraham's faith in Genesis 15 makes one like Abraham, and one can therefore claim to be Abraham's child.

But this is not Paul's argument. It is not faith itself but what faith *brings* that makes one Abraham's son. Faith brings the *pneuma*, and it is the *pneuma* that creates a connection between Abraham and the gentile believer. Why? Because of the identity of the *pneuma* that these gentiles receive. According to Galatians 4:6, God sends the *pneuma*,

6. See Tappenden, *Resurrection in Paul*.

7. For the argument that the Greek phrase *hoi ek pisteōs* (and similar phrases) means "to be born *out of* or *from* faith," not merely "those having faith," see Hodge, *If Sons, Then Heirs*. For instance, we see the preposition *ek* used to refer to birth out of something in Gal. 4:22: "Abraham had two sons, one out of the enslaved woman and one out of the freewoman."

which he identifies as the *pneuma* of his son, the Messiah, into the hearts of these gentiles in Galatia. This is the only place in Galatians that Paul identifies the *pneuma* beyond just referring to it as *pneuma*. That is, the *pneuma* is not some generic *pneuma* but specifically the Messiah's *pneuma*.

I recall a pastor telling me as a teenager that the thought that Jesus enters into someone's heart was laughable—that this was nothing but a mere symbol or metaphor. I think Paul would disagree. Jesus the Messiah invades the flesh-and-blood bodies of those who trust in him via his own *pneuma*. When gentiles receive the *pneuma* by faith, when this *pneuma* enters into their hearts, they have been infused with the stuff of the Messiah, which now permeates their bodies. Simultaneously, these gentiles are clothed in the Messiah. The Messiah, then, both *envelops* them and *indwells* them.

Understandably, this strikes us as odd. The best analogy that I can come up with is a sponge that one immerses in a pail of water. If held underwater long enough, the porous body of the sponge is filled with water while also being surrounded by it. The water simultaneously enters into the sponge and "enclothes" the sponge. This is close to, if not quite the same thing as, what Paul envisages. I have argued elsewhere, following the lead of Caroline Johnson Hodge and Stanley Stowers, that Paul depends here on the ancient science of his day to depict what happens to Messiah followers.[8] Ancient philosophers argued about all kinds of important things. Perhaps to our surprise, one of the things they argued about was the possibility or impossibility of two things *truly* mixing. Take my example of the sponge and water. One could take that sponge out of the pail and squeeze it hard enough to make all the water drip back into the pail. The two materials, water and sponge, do not truly mix together. Or take a chemical reaction in which two substances are mixed together and transform into a new, third substance. Ancient philosophers wouldn't have considered this a true mixture either, since the first two substances would cease to exist. Could a real mixture ever happen, then?

8. Hodge, *If Sons, Then Heirs*; and Stowers, "'Pauline Participation in Christ.'"

According to Stoic philosophers, the answer is yes, and such a mixture they called *krasis*. This is where this philosophical discussion becomes relevant to Paul (and others): the Stoics thought the supreme example of *krasis* was the mixture of an element they called *pneuma* with other, coarser substances that were made out of the four lower elements of air, fire, earth, and water. So, for instance, the Stoics believed that the soul was made from the material of *pneuma* and that this material perfectly combined (*krasis*) with the elements that made up flesh-and-blood bodies to make an organic unity. *Pneuma* continues to exist as *pneuma*, and flesh as flesh, but they share the same space. The Stoics called this the *interpenetration* of two substances. It's a weird concept, and even ancient people sometimes mocked the Stoics for it. For instance, the philosopher Plutarch says the following: "If [*krasis*] occurs in the way [the Stoics] require, however, it is necessary that the things being mixed get into each other and the same thing be at once encompassed by being in the other and encompass it by being its receptacle."[9]

Plutarch thought the idea that two objects or materials could mix in such a way that one both surrounds and is surrounded by the other was laughable. But note how well this description fits what Paul says in a dense section of Romans 8 that talks about the very substance of the *pneuma*: "But you are not in the flesh; you are in the *pneuma*, since the *pneuma* of God dwells in you. Anyone who does not have the *pneuma* of the Messiah is not part of him. But if the Messiah is in you, though the body is dead because of sin, the *pneuma* is life because of righteousness. If the *pneuma* of him who raised Jesus from the dead dwells in you, he who raised the Messiah from the dead will give life to your mortal bodies also through his *pneuma* that dwells in you" (8:9–11). The first sentence parallels Stoic thinking about *krasis* (whether Paul knows it or not): the Messiah follower is in the *pneuma*; simultaneously, the *pneuma* is in the Messiah follower. Again, the best example I can think of is a sponge (the person) both saturated and surrounded by water (the *pneuma*). Via his *pneuma*, then, the Messiah dwells in his

9. Plutarch, *Against the Stoics* 1078B–C.

followers, and they dwell in him. They are in him and of him, and he is in them. This is no mere external relationship *to* or *with* the Messiah; it is full and intricate and intimate participation *in* the Messiah.

I have been convinced by other scholars that the *pneuma*, God's *pneuma*, the Messiah's *pneuma*, in Paul's mind is not something immaterial but the finest, most perfect form of matter.[10] These arguments depend on ancient Stoic thinking again. Yes, this is controversial to many Paul scholars, not least because classical Christian theology has insisted on the immateriality of God. Such theology insists that God cannot be made up of matter because that would mean God is divisible and subject to change and decay. But that is not how some ancient people thought about the stuff of *pneuma*. Philosophical and scientific reflection on *pneuma* goes back at least to Aristotle, who argued that it was in some way related to a fifth element that made up the cosmos. Whereas previous philosophers had proposed four elements—fire, air, earth, and water—Aristotle conceived of one more element, a heavenly one called *aether*. In Platonic thought all matter was given to change and destruction and was therefore inferior, but Aristotle believed that *aether* was unlike the other four elements. It alone was unchanging, eternal, and divine.[11] For Aristotle, when *aether* interacted with the earthly realm (anything below the moon), it did so as *pneuma*. So *pneuma* did not come from any of the four earthly elements but was *aether* interacting with these four elements. And Aristotle had no problem speaking of *pneuma* both as a body and as matter.[12] Why? Because this stuff was indivisible, unchanging, eternal. It was the absolute best stuff out there!

Paul was neither a Stoic nor a highly trained philosopher. But the basic elements of Platonic and Stoic thinking were the conceptual air that most people in the Greco-Roman world breathed. One would surely be wrong to think that all people today know what quarks and hadrons are, but many of us have a basic understanding of what gravity

10. See especially Engberg-Pedersen, *Cosmology and Self*.

11. Aristotle, *On the Heavens* 1.1–3.

12. Aristotle, *On Spirit* 9.485b6–7. See Bos and Ferwerda, *Aristotle*, and Bos, *Aristotle on God's Life-Generating Power*.

is or what atoms, protons, and neutrons are. So too, it is hard to believe that someone like Paul would not have known how the term *pneuma* was being used more broadly in his day. And, if we can trust Acts on this point, Paul came from the city of Tarsus, a known hotbed of Stoic philosophy. This was his world, even if it is not ours.

Therefore, when Paul spoke of the *pneuma*, he was doing so under the influence not only of the Greek translations of Jewish scriptures but also of the intellectual context of his own day, where *pneuma* was thought to be the best material in the cosmos. In other words, unless he unmistakably signaled that he meant something quite different, his readers would inevitably have heard *pneuma* as those around them were commonly using it: to refer to a type of matter that was eternal and divine. While we cannot know what was in Paul's mind, I would suggest that unless he was a very poor communicator, he would have known he needed to clarify what he meant by *pneuma* if he meant something dramatically different from what most others around him would have meant by the term. Otherwise he would have opened himself up to inevitable misunderstandings.

Here's a comical example from parenting: One day my family and I were driving around the city of Buffalo when my four-year-old daughter yelled out (apropos of absolutely nothing): "I hate Mennonites!" Surprised, we asked her why. Her answer: "Because they are always hurting people." Confused, we asked, "Maggie, we're Mennonites—are we always hurting people?" To which she answered, "Oh, wait, I meant *knights*. I hate knights." Considerable misunderstanding (and then laughter) resulted from my daughter using the word *Mennonite*, a word that in part denotes someone committed to pacifism, to refer to almost its exact opposite, a person whose job is to use violence.

Consequently, when Paul speaks about the *pneuma* entering into people's hearts, as he does in Galatians 4:6 and Romans 5:5 and 2 Corinthians 1:22, or more broadly about those who follow the Messiah receiving the *pneuma* (1 Cor. 2:12; 2 Cor. 5:5), modern readers should take this as materially as possible. The *pneuma* is the material gift from God—it is the presence of God and God's Messiah—that enters into human hearts, the epicenter of human bodies. The holy *pneuma* materially inhabits human bodies (Rom. 8:11; 2 Cor. 6:16, quoting a modified form of Lev. 26:11; cf. 2 Tim. 1:14).[13]

How does all of this relate to non-Jews becoming the seed and sons of Abraham? Paul clarifies for his Galatian readers that the *pneuma* they have received through faith is not just any old *pneuma* and definitely not the *pneuma* of this cosmos (1 Cor. 2:12) but the *pneuma* of God's son, Jesus the Messiah (Gal. 4:6). These gentiles have been infused, therefore, with the unchanging and eternal stuff of the Messiah, who himself became *pneuma* at his resurrection (1 Cor. 15:45; 2 Cor. 3:17–18). By infusing gentiles with the Messiah's *pneuma*, God has intervened in the gentile condition by editing their genetic code, modifying gentile DNA, so to speak. The *pneuma* is a vector inserted into the bodies of gentiles so that they now contain the Messiah's genetic code: anyone united to the Lord is one *pneuma* with him (1 Cor. 6:17).

Just prior to Galatians 4:6, Paul outlines an argument that the Messiah is the seed of Abraham (Gal. 3:16). In this verse Paul connects a messianic passage to Genesis's story about Abraham and Abraham's seed. Throughout Galatians 3, Paul riffs on the narrative of Genesis 15, where God makes a promise to Abraham and Abraham trusts God's promise, having this trust counted as righteousness (Gen. 15:6; cf. Gal. 3:6). Paul has this narrative in mind when he identifies Abraham's seed with the Messiah. Immediately before Abraham trusts God's promise, he complains to God that all God's promises seem to be oblivious to the fact that Abraham still has no child to inherit what God promises to give him. As Abraham puts it, "You have not given to me a seed [*sperma*]" (Gen. 15:3). God responds with yet another promise: "The one who comes out of your belly will inherit you" (15:4).[14] Genesis 15 defines Abraham's seed (*sperma*), therefore, as "the one who comes out of your belly." This phrase occurs in only two other places in Jewish

---

13. Two other Pauline passages use the Greek verb *enoikeō* (to inhabit), but not about the *pneuma*: Col. 3:16 speaks of the word of the Messiah inhabiting people, while 2 Tim. 1:5 speaks of trust (*pistis*) inhabiting people. Both, I think, are closely related to the material indwelling of the *pneuma*.

14. This translation is based on the Hebrew. The LXX translation of Gen. 15:4 reads, "The one who comes out of you." See Thiessen, *Paul and the Gentile Problem*, 125, for a discussion of this textual issue.

scriptures, both of which refer to David's offspring. Once it refers to one of David's sons, who seeks to kill David (2 Sam. 16:11). The other is 2 Samuel 7, where through the prophet Nathan, God promises to David that he will raise up David's seed (*sperma*), "the one who comes forth out of your belly" (7:12). The Hebrew in both passages is the same, potentially creating in Paul's mind a connection between Abraham's seed and David's seed.[15]

If Jesus is the Messiah, then he is not only the seed of David but also the seed of Abraham, whom God promised in Genesis 15. And if gentile believers have the Messiah's *pneuma*, then they have his material in them and are, at the same time, clothed in the Messiah. They are in the Messiah, and the Messiah is in them. They have received an infusion of the Messiah's DNA, so to speak. Consequently, they are now materially, genetically, and genealogically connected not just to the Messiah but also to Abraham. They have undergone divine, pneumatic gene therapy to address the fact that they were previously unrelated to Abraham. Pneumatic therapy is a much more advanced technology for addressing the genealogical gap between Abraham and the gentiles than cosmetic surgery ever could be. Through the *pneuma* and in the Messiah, gentiles have become Abraham's sons and seed.

In summary, Paul's opponents were seeking to forge a connection between gentiles and Abraham through circumcision. For Paul, this is problematic for several reasons. The rite of circumcision addressed only the exterior and modified only the flesh, the *sarx*. It was a fleshly and merely skin-deep effort to address a deeper problem (Gal. 3:2–5). As such, it resulted in nothing more than bodily mutilation (Phil. 3:2). Gentiles had not received the *pneuma* through works of the law, so why would works of the law address something that the *pneuma* had not already? By adding works of the law to the *pneuma*, such people were in effect (although presumably not intentionally) implying that works of the law could do something that the *pneuma* could not, which is, of

15. And perhaps other minds. See, e.g., Matt. 1:1, which refers to Jesus as both the son of David and the son of Abraham. A similarly worded promise occurs in Ps. 132:11 (LXX 131:11): "Yhwh swore a truthful oath to David and he will not reject it: 'Out of the fruit of your belly, I appoint your throne.'"

course, to imply that the Messiah had not fully addressed the gentile condition.

Paul again depends on the physics of his day when he makes this argument. Human flesh was made up of a combination of the four lower elements, and so it was mutable and non-eternal. To place confidence in a practice such as circumcision, then, was to place confidence in something that was passing away. If the Galatians tried to forge a connection to Abraham via circumcision, whatever connection they made, being merely skin deep, would simply not stand up to the test of eschatological time. They were making themselves Abrahamic sons according to the flesh (Gal. 4:29), at best citizens of the "now Jerusalem," a terrestrial and therefore non-eternal citizenship in a Jerusalem that would not exist in the eschaton (4:25). In contrast, gentiles who became connected to Abraham through the Messiah's *pneuma* were Abraham's sons according to the *pneuma* (4:29), connected to Abraham via an unchanging, indestructible, eternal material, and therefore were citizens of the Jerusalem above, the celestial and eternal Jerusalem (4:25).

To outline Paul's argument succinctly:

Gentiles need to become Abraham's sons and seed to inherit God's promises.

The Messiah is Abraham's son and seed.

Gentiles, through faith, receive the Messiah's essence, his *pneuma*.

Through faith and *pneuma* they have been placed *into* the Messiah.

The *pneuma* of the Messiah also infuses their bodies.

They have the Messiah's essence in them, and they exist in the essence of the Messiah.

Gentiles have become Abrahamic sons and seed.

9

The Bodies of the Messiah

Becoming genealogically connected to Abraham via the Messiah's *pneuma* not only enables non-Jews to inherit the many things God promised to Abraham; it also now gives new shape to their identity and lives. They have become sons and seed of Abraham through the Messiah. And they have become filled with the *pneuma* of the Jewish Messiah, ordering their lives in fundamentally Jewish ways even as their flesh-and-blood bodies remain non-Jewish.

I wish Paul had written a full treatise on Christology, but he did not. So is it any wonder that scholars remain divided on whether Paul's letters provide evidence of an early "high Christology," which would identify Jesus with Israel's supreme God, or an early "low Christology," in which Jesus would be elevated to a divinity only after his death, or something in between? Paul was not a trinitarian, but do his writings perhaps inevitably point in trinitarian directions? Classic texts such as Romans 9:4–5, where Paul speaks of the Messiah and concludes by saying, "The one who is over all things, God blessed forever," remain contested battlefields. Does the word *God* refer here to the Messiah, or is Paul ending his description of the many blessings that still belong to fleshly Israel, including the Messiah, and then praising Israel's God?

Other texts in Paul's letters seem to imply that the Messiah existed prior to his birth and provide proof of his being divine. For instance, Paul says that at the right time God sent his son, who was born of a woman and under the law was a Jew (Gal. 4:4). God could *send* his son only if he existed prior to his birth. And Paul tells his readers in Corinth that when Israel was wandering in the wilderness after coming out of Egypt, they drank out of the pneumatic rock that followed them (1 Cor. 10:1–4). Here Paul refers to the rock that provided water to Israel at least twice (Exod. 17:5–6; Num. 20:8–11), a popular tradition in Jewish thinking (Deut. 8:15; Neh. 9:15; Pss. 78:20; 105:41; 114:8; Isa. 48:21; Wis. 11:4). Paul claims, though, that this pneumatic rock was actually the Messiah (1 Cor. 10:4). Some interpreters have taken this passage to be an instance of Paul allegorizing, but again that is not at all the case. He does not say, after all, that this rock *is* the Messiah but says it *was* the Messiah. The Messiah, long before he was born in a flesh-and-blood body, existed and became embodied in a rock that provided *pneumatic* sustenance to Israel in the wilderness. The Messiah's petrification preceded his incarnation. Ancient divinities had this ability to take on different bodies.[1] So the Messiah for Paul was a divine being of some sort even before his enfleshment as a human.

At a critical point in Israel's deliverance from slavery in Egypt, the Messiah had become embodied in rock. And now in the fullness of time, Paul says, the Messiah has become embodied in a flesh-and-blood body, one born out of a woman and under the law (Gal. 4:4), in order to deliver people from this present evil age (1:4) and from slavery to gods who are not truly gods (4:8). As I noted previously, Paul does not speak much about the life and teachings of Jesus, the period of his enfleshment. In Galatians 4:4, though, he stresses both Jesus's humanity and his Jewishness. And in his preface to the Romans, he stresses that Jesus was a seed, according to the flesh, of David (Rom.

---

1. For a fascinating account, see Sommer, *Bodies of God*. In "'Rock Was Christ,'" I have sought to apply Sommer's work to help make sense of the multiple bodies of the Messiah in 1 Corinthians.

1:3), again a claim that emphasizes Jesus's enfleshed embodiment, Jewishness, and messianic lineage.[2] The longest description we get of the life of Jesus in Paul is found in a hymnic text that Paul likely adopted and adapted for his letter to the people of the city of Philippi. In this letter Paul calls his readers to imitate the model of the Messiah:

> Who, though he was in the form of a god,
>> did not regard equality with a god
>> as something to be seized,
> but emptied himself,
>> taking the form of one enslaved,[3]
>> being born in the likeness of a human.
> And being found in the shape of a human,
>> he humbled himself
>> and became obedient to the point of death—
>> even death on a cross.
> Therefore God also highly exalted him
>> and gave him the name
>> that is above every name,
> so that at the name of Jesus
>> every knee should bend,
>> in heaven and on earth and under the earth,
> and every tongue should confess
>> that Jesus the Messiah is Lord,
>> to the glory of God the Father. (Phil. 2:6–11)[4]

What we see here and elsewhere in Paul's letters is a pattern to the Messiah's life of descent from the celestial realm to the terrestrial realm, from a pneumatic existence to a flesh-and-blood existence, from a divine existence to an existence as an enslaved human. This Messiah

---

2. On Jesus's messiahship in Paul, see Novenson, *Christ among the Messiahs*.

3. Nijay Gupta ("To Whom Was Christ a Slave?") makes the convincing case that this form of enslavement is the human condition, enslaved under the powers of sin and death.

4. My translation here shows where *theos* is used without the definite article, translating these occurrences as "a god," and shows where *theos* is used with the article, translating these occurrences as "God." I do this not because I am certain that Paul intends to distinguish between Jesus and Israel's God, a lower divinity and the supreme divinity, but to show that this interpretation is possible.

descended so far, humbled himself so much, that he even suffered death on a Roman cross, the most ignoble way to die in the Roman world. Paul no doubt intended readers to contrast this depiction of the Messiah with Adam and Eve, who take forbidden fruit because they believe it will make them equal to gods/God (Gen. 3:5). He might also have expected readers to contrast the Messiah's model here to gods who grasp instead of serve, whether the sons of God in Genesis 6 (and related tales) or stories of various Greco-Roman deities. As a result of the Messiah's willingness to obey and humble himself, the Jewish God raised him from the dead and exalted him back to the celestial realm, above all other names, where he again exists as *pneuma* (see 2 Cor. 3:17; 1 Cor. 15:45) and will be confessed by all powers celestial, terrestrial, and subterranean (Phil. 2:10).

Paul concludes by claiming that the Messiah Jesus is *Lord* (*kyrios*). David Litwa notes that Paul tells a brief story about Jesus in these words from Philippians 2:6-11: "In the brief compass of this passage, Jesus is both hominified and deified. He could be *hominified* because, historically speaking, some Christians as early as the 40s CE identified Jesus with a preexistent divine being endowed with God's form and glory (Phil. 2:6). In the hymn, Jesus is also *deified* by being exalted, worshipped, and receiving 'the name above every name'—all of which are honors properly belonging to Yahweh (here called 'the Father')."[5]

If one were to reconstruct a life of Jesus just from Paul's letters, one would have the following outline: the Messiah or son of God preexisted his birth, was born of a Jewish woman, and belonged to the tribe of Judah. He then was crucified and died, but the Jewish God raised him from the dead and established him over all other powers and names.[6] Not once does Paul mention any deeds of power Jesus does, which the later Gospels emphasize. Just once does Paul *maybe* refer to a legal position of Jesus: his position that people should not seek divorces, and if they do, they definitely should not remarry (1 Cor. 7:10-11). At other places scholars have detected possible evidence that Paul knew

5. Litwa, *Iesus Deus*, 5-6.
6. See here D. Campbell, "Story of Jesus."

other things Jesus taught,[7] but it is illuminating that Paul never feels the need to say, "As Jesus commanded." Paul dwells briefly on the enfleshment of the preexisting Messiah, but his focus is on the death of the Messiah and his victorious resurrection and exaltation. This is where the Messiah's significance lies for Paul.

The Messiah existed prior to his taking on a flesh-and-blood body. He lived (an undetermined amount of time) as a Jewish man from the tribe of Judah. He was crucified, died, and was buried. But on the third day after his death, God raised him from the dead. He appeared to numerous people after this: Peter, then to all the twelve disciples, then to five hundred Messiah followers, then to James, then to all the Messiah's envoys, and *finally* to Paul himself (1 Cor. 15:1–8). Whether Paul believed this resurrection was a resurrection of Jesus's flesh-and-blood body is uncertain, despite N. T. Wright's efforts,[8] though it is possible. What *is* clear, though, is that regardless of how Jesus was *initially* raised, he *no longer* has a flesh-and-blood body: "The Lord is *pneuma*," Paul tells his Corinthian readers (2 Cor. 3:17–18).

In his earlier letter to them, Paul informs the Corinthians that the last Adam, the Messiah, became a "life-giving *pneuma*" (1 Cor. 15:45). Against so many misunderstandings, to say that Jesus has become a *pneuma* is not the same thing as saying that he is now bodiless or immaterial. Remember, for Paul and for his initial readers, *pneuma* was material—the best material available because it was unchanging and eternal. So to claim that the Messiah became a life-giving *pneuma* and to say that he no longer has a flesh-and-blood body is not the same as saying the Messiah no longer has a body or that the resurrection was not bodily. The body of the Messiah in the heavenly realm is a pneumatic body—it consists of the best matter: matter that

7. One possible example is Paul's instructions about eating food in Rom. 14, which use the same word (*koinos*) that Jesus uses in the Gospels about food (e.g., Mark 7:1–19). I think it more likely, though, that Mark knows Rom. 14.

8. Wright, *Resurrection of the Son of God*. To be sure, both Luke and John depict Jesus's fleshly resurrection. In John 20:24–29 the resurrected Jesus still bears the fleshly wounds of his crucifixion, and in Luke 24:39 Jesus tells his disciples to touch him and see that he is not a *pneuma*, since *pneuma* does not have flesh (*sarx*) and bones. Whether either of these Gospel writers believed Jesus ascended to heaven where he continues to have a flesh-and-blood body, though, is uncertain. See Heim, "In Heaven as on Earth?"

is glorious, powerful, heavenly, indestructible, and immortal (1 Cor. 15:41–43, 47–48, 53–54).

Already in the second century CE, many Christians no longer shared with Paul the belief that *pneuma* was material and so sought to reread Paul. One can see this discomfort in the brazen effort of the person who penned 3 Corinthians in Paul's name, completely undermining Paul's own argument in 1 Corinthians 15. While Christians of later generations may not share Paul's physics, they should not seek to reinvent him in their own image. Let Paul be Paul, no matter how weird he gets.[9]

As I noted in the preceding chapter, Paul believed that *pneuma* was material and was a type of body, following one prevalent scientific theory of his day.[10] Paul's physics differed from later classical Christian theology, and this might be an uncomfortable realization for some readers. Again, classical Christian theology stipulates that God cannot have a body and must not consist of matter precisely because all matter is subject to change and decay and destruction. With those scientific assumptions in place, classical Christian theologians necessarily had to conclude that God could not have a body or be made up of matter. The supreme God must be eternal, indestructible, and immortal. So because God is *pneuma* (Christian theologians couldn't just do away with John 4:24, which states concisely that God is *pneuma*), they came to define *pneuma* as immaterial and bodiless. Paul and classical Christian theology disagree on whether *pneuma* is material and makes up a body, but they agree on some essential things: God, as *pneuma*, is not subject to decay or destruction. God, as *pneuma*, is eternal and immortal.

9. On one effort to grapple honestly with Paul's foreign thinking while seeking to retain its theological value, see Padgett, "Body in Resurrection."

10. Some early Christian theologians still subscribed to Stoic science here. For instance, in the early third century CE, Tertullian says the following: "In what form of God? Evidently in some form, not in none: for who will deny that God is body, although God is a spirit? For spirit is body, of its own kind, in its own form" (*Against Praxeas* 7; trans. Evans). And while disagreeing with them, Origen notes that some Christians have understood references to God as fire or *pneuma* to be proof of God's embodiment: "Many have produced lengthy discussions of God and his essence. Some have even said that he has a bodily nature which is composed of fine particles and is like ether" (*Commentary on the Gospel according to John* 13.123; trans. Heine; cf. *First Principles* 1.1.1; trans. Butterworth).

And this is what the Messiah has become after his resurrection. As a fully pneumatic being, the Messiah *now* has the ability to be present or to be embodied in multiple ways at the same time. So Paul can speak of God exalting the Messiah over all things (Phil. 2:9), a statement that speaks to his ascension to the heavenly realm, and Paul also can envisage the Messiah being simultaneously present in other ways. This is the heart of Paul's theology: the bodies of the Messiah. The risen and exalted and pneumatic Messiah also has an earthly body, and one needs to be a part of it or even *in* it. Over seventy times Pauline literature uses the Greek phrase *en Christō*, "in the Messiah." A century ago, Albert Schweitzer argued that "'being-in-Christ' is the prime enigma of the Pauline teaching: once grasped it gives the clue to the whole."[11] He labels this aspect of Paul's thinking his *mysticism*. Although many people claim that E. P. Sanders is the founder of the new perspective on Paul, his actual treatment of Paul restates much of Schweitzer's important argument, albeit using the language of *real participation* and not *mysticism*.[12]

Both terms have their limitations: What does *mysticism* mean? What does *participation* mean? To my mind, the best treatment of the concept of being in the Messiah is the often-overlooked work of Caroline Johnson Hodge, who argues that one needs to think in bodily and biological terms. Do not treat this language abstractly; rather, understand

---

11. Schweitzer, *Mysticism of Paul the Apostle*, 3. The question is whether we have fully grasped it. Recent efforts to wrestle with "in Messiah" language in Paul include Hewitt, *Messiah and Scripture*, and Morgan, *Being "in Christ."*

12. Misunderstandings of Sanders abound, unfortunately. Sanders provided a new perspective on Judaism—it was not a religion of works righteousness; ancient Jews believed their God was gracious. This new perspective *on Judaism* (although others had made similar claims earlier) was then picked up first by N. T. Wright and used to provide a new perspective on Paul in Wright's 1978 Tyndale Lecture and unpublished 1981 Oxford dissertation, "The Messiah and the People of God: A Study in Pauline Theology with Particular Reference to the Argument of the Epistle to the Romans" (and subsequent publications). James D. G. Dunn did likewise, popularizing the term in a 1983 article titled "The New Perspective on Paul." Dunn and Wright have continued to use the terminology. Both have argued that Paul contested Judaism not because it was a religion of works righteousness but because it was ethnocentric. My own sense is that Wright's emphasis on this point has lessened over the years. Dunn, though, never stopped characterizing (and caricaturing) ancient Judaism as ethnocentric.

it in terms of bodies or containers.[13] The Messiah is a receptacle that contains the bodies of his followers. They are enveloped by the Messiah's *pneuma* and are therefore materially *in* the Messiah. Most significantly, the Messiah continues to have a flesh-and-blood body, not in the heavenly realm where it could not survive but in the earthly realm. And this body is a little more complicated than the earthly body the Messiah had when he first took on flesh. Now his body consists of numerous flesh-and-blood bodies: male and female, enslaved and free, Jew and non-Jew. The Messiah's body contains a multitude of body parts, consisting of different genders, ethnicities, and social strata.

It is natural for modern readers to understand Paul to be speaking "merely metaphorically" (whatever that means), but to do so is to make Paul sensible to our minds, not to let him speak his own. Paul thinks that the Jewish God has taken all sorts of flesh-and-blood human bodies and knit them together into an organic whole: the body of the Messiah. The Messiah's followers are his flesh-and-blood body on earth. They are immersed in the Messiah. They are clothed in the Messiah. They all have become one in the Messiah (Gal. 3:26–28). Paul describes believers as the Messiah's body most fully in 1 Corinthians 12, but he does so also in Romans 12:4–8. In both letters he emphasizes diversity as necessary to bodily health and integrity.

The Stoics could use body language for numerous types of things. So they could speak of a group of soldiers or a murder of crows or a cauldron of bats or a pace of donkeys as a *body*. No Stoic thought that such bodies were organically connected like a single sheep's body. And they could use the term *body* to speak of things constructed from different objects, like a house or a ship. Again, no Stoic would have thought of such things as organically connected. When they did speak of an organically connected body, they signaled this by identifying the presence of *pneuma*, which functioned in Stoic thinking as the ontological glue that fused disparate things together into a single organic body.[14]

---

13. Hodge, *If Sons, Then Heirs*. See also Stowers, "'Pauline Participation in Christ.'" On the language of containers, see Tappenden, *Resurrection in Paul*.

14. See the important work of Michelle Lee, *Paul, the Stoics, and the Body of Christ*.

The idea that Messiah followers constitute, both individually and most fully together, the Messiah's earthly flesh-and-blood body must have been a sobering thought. What one does with one's body is what one does with the Messiah's body. For this reason Paul stresses to the Corinthians that although they have now become infused with the Messiah's *pneuma*, they are still flesh-and-blood and that flesh-and-blood matters. Why? Because the flesh-and-blood body functions in the same way that a brick-and-mortar temple does. It is a receptacle for the sacred presence of God. Again, this idea of the body as a temple is both corporate (the bodies of *all* Messiah followers make up one temple) and individual (the body of *each* Messiah follower is also a temple). We see Paul emphasizing the corporate aspect of the body-temple in the following passage: "Do you all not know that you all are God's temple and that God's *pneuma* dwells in you? If anyone destroys God's temple, God will destroy that person. For God's temple is holy, and you all are that temple" (1 Cor. 3:16–17).[15]

A few chapters later, Paul combines the corporate body and the individual body. What one does with one's individual body one does with the corporate body of the Messiah. Responding to his concern that some of the Messiah followers in Corinth are using their flesh-and-blood bodies for sexually immoral behavior, Paul stresses that even though these types of bodies are obsolete in comparison to what they will one day have, they still need to be used properly because they currently function as sacred space: "Or do you all not know that your [plural] body [singular!] is a temple of the holy *pneuma* within you all, which you all have from God, and that you all are not your own? For you all were bought with a price; therefore glorify God in your [plural] body [singular]" (1 Cor. 6:19–20).[16]

I should stress that referring to flesh-and-blood human bodies as God's temple does *not* negate the importance of the Jerusalem temple. As Paula Fredriksen notes, "Paul praises the new community by

15. I have used "you all" here to show where the Greek is plural.
16. This is related to but distinct from Seneca, Paul's contemporary, who states, "Unless the soul be pure and holy, there is no room in it for God" (*Moral Epistles* 87.21). Paul emphasizes the purity of the body, Seneca the purity of the soul.

likening it to something that he values supremely. Had he valued the temple less, he would not have used it to exemplify his communities; if he had challenged the function and probity of the laws of sacrifice, he would not have used them as the binding metaphor for his mission."[17] Nor, for that matter, does it signify that Paul thinks the Jerusalem temple no longer houses Israel's God. People in the ancient Mediterranean world, including many ancient Jews, believed their gods could frequently become embodied in more than one body at a time. Israel's God, after all, dwelled in the temple but also in heaven. Paul could just as easily have believed that God inhabited the Jerusalem temple, dwelled in heaven, and dwelled in the Messiah's followers.[18]

17. Fredriksen, *Sin*, 38.
18. For a thorough treatment of the long and varied history of the idea that God could dwell in bodies, making them his temple(s), see Harrington, *Purity and Sanctuary of the Body*. From a more theological perspective, see Wyschogrod, *Body of Faith*.

10

Living the Resurrected Life

Paul's message focuses on Jesus, who descended from David and who was declared God's son with power at his resurrection (Rom. 1:3–4). And Paul believed that in the incarnation, death, and resurrection of this particular and peculiar *son* of God, a whole new generation of *sons* of God *had* come and *would be* coming into existence. The Messiah, a Jewish eschatological figure, had been raised from the dead, a common (but not universal) Jewish eschatological hope. And humans becoming angelic or divine themselves was also a common Jewish expectation. Paul's thinking remained Jewish, but he was faced with a wrinkle. The resurrection had started with one person, Jesus, but had not transformed the rest of the cosmos in the thoroughgoing way that most would have anticipated. Instead, he and other Messiah followers were living in an increasingly odd period where the resurrection had begun and was beginning to work in them but was far from fully manifest.

Paul himself serves as a prime example of this new existence, claiming that the Messiah now lives *inside* him (Gal. 2:20). If the son of God lives inside Paul, it follows that Paul too must be a son of God. This is a claim he makes: those whom God's *pneuma* leads are sons of God, and they will one day be revealed to the cosmos as such (Rom. 8:14, 19). Even non-Jews will be called sons of the living God, something Paul thinks the prophet Hosea predicted long ago (Rom. 9:26; LXX Hosea 2:1). How? Like Paul, those who are both clothed in and inhabited by the Messiah are sons of God (Gal. 3:26). Being in the Messiah means having the Messiah, who is God's son (Gal. 4:6), in and through the indwelling presence of the *pneuma* of the Messiah.[1] People infected or invaded or possessed by the Messiah's *pneuma* are now God's sons, and they call out to God, naming him *Abba*, Father.[2]

Paul claims in his letter to the Romans that God conforms believers to the image (*eikōn*) of his son. The Messiah, Paul tells his readers, is the firstborn among many brothers (8:29). While the NRSVue's efforts to be gender inclusive may be admirable, its translation of *pollois adelphois* as "a large family" is unhelpful in that it obscures the fact that, *as brothers*, Paul's readers are also sons of God. The creation of new sons of God explains Paul's pervasive use of familial language: Paul begins his letters to Rome, Corinth (not 2 Corinthians), and Thessalonica (cf. Colossians) by calling his readers *adelphoi*, and he addresses them throughout these and other letters in fraternal terms.[3] Why? Because they truly are brothers, a new genus of humans who are sons of God, related to one another through their pneumatic connection to God's son and ultimately to Israel's God.

This language must be understood within the larger Jewish tradition, since the Pentateuch and other sacred texts refer to lower deities as "the sons of God" (Hebrew: *bene ha-elohim* or *bene elim*; Greek: *hoi huioi tou theou* or *huioi theou*).[4] Many later Jewish texts defuse some of these polytheistic passages by calling these lower deities "angels."[5]

1. Hodge, *If Sons, Then Heirs*; Stowers, "'Pauline Participation in Christ.'"
2. On being possessed by the Messiah's *pneuma*, see Bazzana, *Having the Spirit of Christ*.
3. The thirteen letters attributed to Paul use *adelph-* language 139 times. Paul also uses *teknon* or *teknion* in Rom. 8:16–17, 21; 9:8; Phil. 2:15.
4. Gen. 6:2–4; Job 1:6; 2:1; 38:7; Pss. 29:1 (LXX 28:1); 89:7 (LXX 88:7).
5. E.g., the LXX translator of Job renders the Hebrew as "angels." Some Greek manuscripts of Genesis also render *bene ha-elohim* in Gen. 6:2–4 as "angels." Cf. 1 Enoch 6, Jubilees 5, and Testament of Solomon 5.3. Other later Jewish texts continue to use the

But this polytheism needs to be understood as still seeing one supreme God ruling over lower gods, who are sometimes called angels.

Paul and the Holy Ones

Paul uses language of Messiah followers that identifies them with angelic beings. Frequently, Paul refers to those in the Messiah as *hoi hagioi*.[6] Modern translators unhelpfully translate the term as "the saints," thereby evoking images of haloed humans such as Francis or Patrick, Joan or Teresa. But how would first-century readers have understood this term? Jewish writers, especially in poetic works, frequently used the phrase "the holy ones" to speak of lower divinities. The Song of Moses, for instance, depicts God as glorious among the holy ones (Exod. 15:11), and Deuteronomy refers to God coming from Sinai with thousands of holy ones (33:2–3). The book of Job also refers to the holy ones, something the LXX translator renders as "holy angels" (5:1). Confusingly, the Psalter calls both God's people (15:3; 33:10) and lower deities (88:6, 8) "the holy ones." And Zechariah depicts God coming with all his holy ones (14:5).

Early Jewish writers continue in this usage. According to Ben Sira, God made Moses equal in glory to the holy ones (Sir. 45:2). The high priest Simon, according to the author of 3 Maccabees, claims that God is holy "among the holy ones" (3:2, 21). The author of Jude, quoting 1 Enoch 1.9, says, "See, the Lord is coming with ten thousand of his holy ones" (14). And the Wisdom of Solomon equates the holy ones with the sons of God, asking about the fate of the righteous:

> Why have they been numbered among the sons of God?
> And why is their lot among the holy ones? (5:5)

---

language of "sons of God" with no apparent concern for some (modern) conception of what monotheism must look like. See, e.g., Pseudo-Philo 3.1; Prayer of Joseph 1.6. On this polytheism, see M. Smith, *Origins of Biblical Monotheism*.

6. Rom. 1:7; 8:27; 12:13; 15:25, 26, 31; 16:2, 15; 1 Cor. 1:2; 6:1, 2; 7:14; 14:33; 16:1, 15; 2 Cor. 1:1; 8:4; 9:1, 12; 13:12; Phil. 1:1; 4:22; Philem. 5, 7. In the disputed letters: Eph. 1:1, 15, 18; 2:19; 3:8, 18; 4:12; 5:3; 6:18; Col. 1:2, 4, 12, 26; 2 Thess. 1:10; 1 Tim. 5:10.

But the most concentrated usage of "holy ones" language is attested in the various scrolls discovered at Qumran, where we see the phrase used almost a hundred times in numerous works.[7] The evidence suggests that the phrase can apply both to Israel and to God's divine council or his angels and likely implies that the boundaries between some humans and angels were both fuzzy and porous.

At the very least, then, when Paul calls believers "holy ones," he signals that they are a people set apart for God. But there are reasons to believe that Paul also thinks that these holy ones and sons of God are *humans* who are in the process of becoming *angelic*. Paul makes a telling exegetical sleight of hand in his quotation of Zechariah 14:5, which refers to God's eschatological coming with his holy ones (1 Thess. 3:13). In the context of Zechariah, these holy ones are angelic beings who accompany God into battle to deliver Israel. But if Paul's use of *hagioi* throughout his letters is indicative, his reference to holy ones in 1 Thessalonians 3:13 must refer to those in the Messiah. Why has Paul swapped out God's divine beings for humans? Because he thinks that believers in Jesus participate in his divinity even as they await the resurrection, when they will become fully divine. Paul has good precedent for this erasure of the line between angel and human since Zechariah had already predicted the collapse of these categories, predicting that the house of David will be like gods, like the angel of Yhwh himself (Zech. 12:8).

At God's coming, then, God's people will be made divine or angelic. For Paul, this is already happening in his mission as the Messiah's herald. Those in the Messiah have taken on a divine identity already, but it is one that is, for the most part, hidden. It will, nonetheless, be fully manifested in the future and should dictate how those in the Messiah behave morally here and now.

The Angelic Rule of the Messiah and His People

In Romans 1, Paul details the agonizing spiral of gentiles into idolatry and immorality. The catalyst, as he so poignantly puts it, was their

---

7. For the angelology of Qumran, see Walsh, *Angels Associated with Israel*.

decision to swap the glory of the *immortal* God for images of *mortal* beings (1:23). Because humans mimic what they worship, a consequence of this ill-advised trade is that *now* they lack God's glory (3:23), having themselves become more like the mortal things they worship—enslaved to the needs and desires inherent to mortality. Their idolatry has led to immorality, the consequence of which is death or mortality (1:32). If you worship lifeless images of beings who are themselves subject to death, then you will inevitably produce dead and worthless deeds, only to then die yourself.

While Romans 1 details this death spiral, Paul later argues that the origins of sin and death go back to the first human, Adam: "Sin entered the cosmos through one person, and death entered through sin, and in this way death passed into all humans" (Rom. 5:12). Paul's point is that sin and death existed even prior to the law that taught what sin was: even though there was no Mosaic law, death still ruled from Adam to Moses. Romans 5, then, suggests that death's dominion extended to all humanity, even though Paul's rhetorical focus here is not on the law or Moses or Israel. Rather, he merely seeks to establish that, even apart from the law, gentiles had suffered the consequences of sin and found themselves under death's rule. The law-free existence of gentiles did not preclude them from the consequences of sin and from the powerful reign of death.

But, as Paul elsewhere spells out, in the wake of his ambassadorship on behalf of the Messiah Jesus—a new ruler who supplants death's dominion—gentiles are being brought back to life (Rom. 6). The message about the Messiah has turned gentiles away from enslavement to idols, those images of mortal things, to a new enslavement to the living God (1 Thess. 1:9). The new reign of the Messiah that Paul heralds, a reign that results in gentiles submitting to and loyally obeying both the resurrected Messiah and the living God, leads to eternal life (Rom. 5:21). This eternal life, while only fully enjoyed in the future, courses through the veins of believers now, as ought to be evident in their moral lives.

Previously morally corrupt and ethically bankrupt gentiles, incapable of pulling themselves up by their moral bootstraps, have received

a gift of incomparable worth and power: Israel's God has infused them
with the equivalent of moral steroids. They did not deserve it, and
they did not earn it through anything they had done. But they desperately needed it. Through the message about the Messiah Jesus,
God has invested these morally weak people with a treasure: the holy
pneuma (Gal. 3:1–5). Paul describes this *pneuma* in numerous ways: it
is the *pneuma*, the holy *pneuma*, the *pneuma* of holiness, the *pneuma* of
God, the *pneuma* of (God's) son, and the *pneuma* of the Messiah. These
various descriptions point to the shape of life in which those loyal to
the Messiah now participate both individually and corporately.

Paul makes it clear that the glorious future of those in the Messiah includes reigning over the cosmos (Rom. 4:13), lower divinities
included; even now neither angels nor rulers nor powers can separate
believers from God's love (Rom. 8:38). And God will soon crush the
malevolent deity, the Satan, under the feet of believers (Rom. 16:20),
a likely allusion to both Genesis 3:15 and Psalm 8:6 (cf. Ps. 110:1). If
Paul has the latter verse in mind, Satan is identified as one of the
angels that will be under the feet of humanity. At the end, believers
will be elevated even above the angels, judging the cosmos and the old
order of angels (1 Cor. 6:2–3). The *new* sons of God that Paul's mission
has given birth to will one day rule over even older sons of God. With
the Messiah, they will reign. According to Paul's good news, multiple
new and superior gods are coming into existence, and even formerly
godless and immoral non-Jews can ascend to the stars (see the next
chapter). This does not threaten Paul's belief in one supreme God; it
rather confirms it. The supreme God is God by nature (*physis*) and has
the power to deify others. All other gods are gods only by God's gift
or grace, a gift that is newly available to humanity in and through the
Messiah and the Messiah's *pneuma*.[8]

8. Some Christian readers may balk at the idea that Paul believes in many gods and
deification. But theologians since (at least) Origen have had no problem conceiving of
multiple gods under the supreme God. For instance, Origen, *Homilies on Exodus* 6.5: "The
words 'Who is like you among the gods?' . . . means those gods who by grace and participation in God are called Gods" (on Exod. 15:11; trans. Heine). On the modern theological
distinction between the God who is supreme and who is God by nature (*physis*) and gods
who are gods by participation or gift (*charis*), see Tanner, *Christ the Key*.

A Holy Life out of a Holy Identity

The gift of the *pneuma* infuses Jesus's followers with an essence and force that empowers them to live holy lives, a central theme in Pauline letters, both undisputed and disputed, which use the adjective *holy* (*hagios*) seventy-six times.[9] Messiah followers have been made holy, they are called holy ones, and they must now live holy lives. Paul gives numerous lists of virtues—for instance, the fruit of the *pneuma* who inhabits them (Gal. 5:22–23).

As Jacob Milgrom has argued, in the priestly writings now preserved in the Pentateuch, holiness has to do with life.[10] We see this same association in Paul's letters with regard to the holy *pneuma*. Paul tells his readers in Rome that it is the *pneuma* of holiness that raised Jesus from the dead (Rom. 1:4; 8:11), and he refers to the *pneuma* as the *pneuma* of life (8:2, 10), who sets believers free from sin and death so that they might themselves live (8:13). The *pneuma*'s mind or purpose or will is life, so setting one's mind on what belongs to the *pneuma* is life (8:6). Paul claims that the resurrected Jesus has himself become a life-giving *pneuma* (1 Cor. 15:45). And in 2 Corinthians he speaks of the *pneuma* of the living God who makes alive (3:3–6), while in Galatians, Paul claims that sowing to the *pneuma* results in reaping eternal life (6:8). For Paul, and in keeping with Israel's priestly thinking, holiness is equated with or leads to life (Rom. 6:22), so the presence and work of the holy *pneuma* inevitably leads to life.

Conversely, sin and death are closely intertwined, precisely because sin is connected to impurity, which is a force of death. Sin, or *moral impurity*, results in death (Rom. 6:16, 23).[11] Obeying God results in righteousness, which in turn results in being made holy (6:19). "Therefore, do not let sin rule in your mortal body so that you obey its passions. Do not offer your body parts as weapons of injustice to sin; rather, offer yourselves to God as those being alive from the dead, and your body

9. Galatians never uses the language of holiness.
10. Milgrom, "Dynamics of Purity."
11. Rom. 5:12, 14, 21; 7:5, 13; 8:2; 1 Cor. 15:56.

parts as weapons of justice to God. For sin will not rule you" (6:12–14).[12] Paul was convinced that followers of the Messiah were destined for the stars. He had no worries about having otherworldly goals—such were quite common in the ancient Mediterranean world both inside and outside Jewish circles.[13] But this did not mean that the terrestrial realm held no interest for him. In actuality, he had to fight off this potential misapplication of his teachings in his letters to those in Corinth, who thought that because their flesh-and-blood bodies were insignificant compared to their pneumatic-ness, it did not matter what they did with their flesh and blood.

Being in the Messiah unplugs a person from the power of sin and death. Why? In the Messiah, fleshly humans are infused with the holy *pneuma* of life, a force of power, a law even, that is stronger than the law of sin and death. Although the sin and flesh proved too powerful for the Jewish law, they were not strong enough to resist and overcome the *pneuma* that God gives (Rom. 8:2–3). Now the *pneuma of God* dwells in the bodies of Messiah followers (8:9). This is the same *pneuma* of the same God who displayed his power over death by raising the crucified Jesus. If the *pneuma* raised Jesus from the dead, this *pneuma* could just as easily give life, here meaning life-giving moral power, to the mortal bodies of flesh in which it dwells (8:11). Just as Paul used the verb of dwelling (*oik-*) three times in relation to sin inhabiting the body, now he uses this verb of dwelling three times in relation to the *pneuma*'s dwelling in bodies. The *pneuma* overwhelms and overcomes sin and death by rewiring the human constitution so that it can now live a holy life. The "gene therapy" of the *pneuma* also infuses Messiah followers with a new moral power.

The Messiah's followers remain flesh-and-blood bodies: frail, mortal, corruptible. Yet now these fleshy people are also filled with the life-giving, empowering, holy *pneuma* of God.[14] They are dirt bodies

---

12. Similarly, 1 Thess. 4:7: "For God did not call us to [*epi*] impurity but in [*en*] holiness" (NRSVue).

13. See Long, *Immortality in Ancient Philosophy*.

14. Other places where the *pneuma* of God or the *pneuma* of the Messiah dwells in the bodies of humans in Paul: 1 Cor. 3:16; 2 Cor. 6:16. In disputed letters we see this theme as well. The Messiah dwells in the hearts of the Messiah's followers (Eph. 3:9), and the

inhabited by the sacred *pneuma*, or as Paul says in 2 Corinthians, "We have this treasure in clay jars" (4:7). It seems like a mismatch since one does not generally put immeasurably valuable items in cardboard boxes. But God has done this to show that the moral power that the Messiah's followers have comes not out of their own beings, clay vessels that they are, but from his presence within them.

There is, though, a struggle within the bodies of Messiah followers since the flesh still exists. The flesh and *pneuma* oppose one another (Gal. 5:16–17), but Paul believes that the *pneuma* should win. It is a more powerful force, after all. Messiah followers now have the freedom and power to live the holy lives, the freedom and power that they previously lacked when sin enslaved their flesh. Now they can choose between the two. This is not necessarily an automatic thing or "robo-righteousness," as Christine Hayes puts it, but it is (or it ought to be, in Paul's mind) quite close to it.[15] There is simply no reason that Messiah followers should sin. They should want to choose the good, the holy, the just, and they should be able to do so now that the holy *pneuma* animates them.[16]

Of course, Paul's various letters are telling evidence that the earliest Messiah followers frequently did not live the lives he thought they were empowered to live. But Paul nonetheless expected them to do so. The *pneuma* is like moral steroids, giving new power to the otherwise morally frail flesh-and-blood body.

---

fullness of God dwelled in the Messiah (Col. 1:19; 2:9). And 2 Tim. 1:14 says, "Guard the good treasure entrusted to you, with the help of the Holy Spirit living in us" (NRSVue).

15. Hayes, *What's Divine about Divine Law?*, 48.

16. See Boakye, *Death and Life*.

11

Resurrection as the Culmination of the Messiah's Coming

What is the good news? First and foremost, it is a message about God's son (Rom. 1:9), the Messiah (1 Cor. 9:12). But what makes this message about Jesus *good* news? Many readers of Paul might be tempted to say that the good news is that Jesus died so that God could forgive the sins of humanity. Paul does indeed say things like this, but it is striking how infrequently he does. One of the few places where he explicitly links Jesus's death to human sins is 1 Corinthians 15:3: "The Messiah died *for* our sins according to the scriptures." Yet shortly after this, Paul claims that if Jesus's death were the end of the story, then his readers' loyalty to Jesus would be empty, and they would still be in their sins (15:17). Jesus's death, in other words, might be necessary, but it alone is insufficient to deal with sins. And in Galatians, Paul claims that the "Messiah gave himself for our sins" (1:4), but here the result is connected not to forgiveness but to liberation from this present evil age. Others have found the idea of Jesus's death atoning for sins in other passages in Paul (e.g., Rom. 3:25). But Paul rarely speaks of *forgiveness* at all. In one central occurrence, he quotes from Psalm 32: "Blessed are those whose lawless deeds are forgiven" (Rom. 4:7, quoting Ps. 32:1, which uses the Greek verb *aphiēmi*). The only other times this verb refers to sins are in disputed letters (Eph. 1:7; Col. 1:4). I point this out not to suggest that Jesus's death is not important for Paul. It obviously is, but it is only a part of a larger narrative that culminates in Jesus's resurrection. Jesus's resurrection gives meaning to his death on the cross. And it is Jesus's resurrection and the way it ripples through the cosmos that matter most to Paul.[1]

Absolutely central to this message about the Messiah is that he died, *but* Israel's God has raised him from the dead (Rom. 1:4). A later writer, under the influence of Paul, puts it this way:

> Remember Jesus the Messiah,
> raised from the dead,
> of the seed of David,
> according to my good news. (2 Tim. 2:8)

Paul claims that this message is God's power to deliver both Jews and non-Jews (Rom. 1:16; cf. Eph. 1:13). This power to deliver relates precisely to resurrection from the dead, rescuing people from the twin powers of sin and death, immorality and mortality. The Pauline tradition makes this clear. According to Ephesians, the good news enables one to share in the promise that is in Jesus the Messiah (3:6), something the author describes as unfathomable riches (3:8). It also leads to obtaining the glory of the Lord Jesus the Messiah (2 Thess. 2:14) and is the good news of the glory of the blessed God (1 Tim. 1:11). Relatedly, through this good news Jesus abolishes death and makes known life and immortality (2 Tim. 1:10).

---

1. See now Moffitt, *Rethinking the Atonement*, which uncovers the logic of death and resurrection in Hebrews especially but has still-to-be-discovered consequences for reading Paul's letters.

The good news, then, is that God has raised Jesus the Messiah from the dead and will enable others to overcome death and share in all the riches that the Messiah now enjoys: glory, life, immortality, resurrection. One can see why Paul would have thought that this was good news.

The verb "to raise" (*egeirō*) occurs forty-one times in the Pauline letters (undisputed and disputed), while the noun "resurrection" (*anastasis*) occurs ten times. For instance, in Romans Paul speaks frequently of the Messiah's resurrection (*anastasis* twice; *egeirō* nine times; *anistēmi* once), while he speaks of the resurrection of believers once. In 1 Corinthians, Paul uses the verb *egeirō* seven times in relation to the Messiah's resurrection and eleven times in relation to the resurrection of believers, and he uses *anastasis* three times of believers. In 2 Corinthians he uses the verb *egeirō* twice of the Messiah and twice of the Messiah's followers. In Galatians he uses *egeirō* once for the Messiah. And he uses *anastasis* of the Messiah once in Philippians (cf. one time in 2 Timothy). First Thessalonians uses *egeirō* language once for the Messiah and once for believers (4:14, 16). Ephesians uses *egeirō* language once of the Messiah and once for believers (1:20; 5:14), as does Colossians. Of the letters ascribed to or written by Paul, only 1 Timothy, Titus, and Philemon make no mention of resurrection explicitly.

In Romans 15, Paul quotes the prophet Isaiah:

> The root of Jesse shall come,
> the one who arises [*ho anistamenos*] to rule the gentiles;
> in him the gentiles shall hope. (Rom. 15:12; LXX Isa. 11:10)

Paul takes this verse to be an ancient prophecy that the Davidic Messiah would rise from the dead and as a result would be given the power to rule the gentiles. This seems more probable when one notes that all but one of the other occurrences of the Greek verb *anistēmi* in Paul's letters refer to the resurrection.[2]

---

2. The only exception is 1 Cor. 10:7, a quotation of the Greek translation of Exod. 32:6.

We can see Paul's story of God's life-giving work outlined succinctly in a few brief sentences in Romans 4. There Paul weaves God's creation of the cosmos, Father Abraham, Jesus, and the life of the Messiah's faithful together into one sweeping narrative of how God acts. In relation to creation, Paul refers to Israel's God as "the one who calls into being the things that are not" (Rom. 4:17; cf. 1 Cor. 1:28). Out of what was not (the Hebrew of Gen. 1:2 speaks of the earth being *tohu ve-bohu*, a phrase that denotes a chaotic mess, not metaphysical nothingness),[3] God brought something—an ordered cosmos in which life could flourish. Abraham trusts in the God who can and has done this, an especially poignant trust given that he and Sarah are defined by what they are not: they are *not* young (Gen. 18:12), they are *not* fruitful (11:30), and they are *not* parents (11:30; 15:2; 16:1). Abraham and Sarah are not good material for becoming parents of many nations (17:5). But God calls the things that are not as though they are, and so even though Abraham, being almost a hundred years old, and Sarah, being almost ninety years old and having a sterile womb, were as good as dead reproductively, Abraham trusted God, who fulfilled the promise to give them seed (Rom. 4:18; Gen. 15:5).[4] Out of as-good-as-dead bodies, God brought new life. This same God acted in the same way in relation to Israel's Messiah. Jesus had been put to death because of human sins, but God raised him from the dead (Rom. 4:24–25; cf. 2 Cor. 1:9; Gal. 1:1; Eph. 1:20; Col. 2:12). And finally, Paul argues, this

3. I am unconvinced that Gen. 1 depicts creation out of absolute nothingness (*creatio ex nihilo*); rather, the point is that God takes things of no account, unruly waters, darkness, *tohu ve-bohu*, and chaotic mess and creates order and a habitat that permits life to flourish. One can see similar sentiments in, e.g., Joseph and Aseneth 12.1–2; 2 Baruch 21.4; 48.8. Philo of Alexandria puts it well: God "has called the things that have no being into being, order out of disorder" (*Special Laws* 4.187).

4. Origen (*Commentary on Romans* 4.7.3; trans. Scheck) believes that Abraham's faith was itself resurrection faith: "For when [Abraham] was commanded to sacrifice his only son, he believed that God was able to raise him from the dead; he believed as well that this matter would not only be accomplished at that time for Isaac but that the full truth of the mystery would be reserved for his seed, who is Christ." Similarly, Origen, *Homilies on Genesis* 8.1 (trans. Heine): "The Apostle, therefore, has reported to us the thoughts of the faithful man, that the faith in the resurrection began to be held already at that time in Isaac. Abraham, therefore, hoped for the resurrection of Isaac and believed in a future which had not yet happened. How, then, are they 'sons of Abraham' who do not believe what has happened in Christ, which Abraham believed was to be in Isaac?"

same God acts in the same way in relation to those who put their trust in this God: they, like Abraham, will be considered just and through Jesus's resurrection will be justified (Rom. 4:22–25; 10:9).

The good news, then, is a movement from death to life because this is how God has acted in the past: at creation and then throughout Israel's history. And this is how God is now acting in the wake of the Messiah's death and will again act in relation to the Messiah's followers. This God is a God of life. This God is the living God (Rom. 9:26; 2 Cor. 3:3; 6:16; cf. 1 Tim. 3:15; 4:10). This God is a God who, when confronted with death, makes life.

Death	Life
Chaos/nothing	Creation
Old/sterile Abraham and Sarah	Isaac → Jacob → Israel
Crucified Jesus	Resurrected Jesus
Dead and sinful humanity	Resurrected and moral humanity

Paul's letters frequently speak of resurrection because this is the heart of his message: Jesus's resurrection, which has just happened, and the imminent resurrection of all those who commit themselves to this good news and find themselves connected to the Messiah's fate (Rom. 6:5, 14; 1 Cor. 15; 2 Cor. 4:13–14). While the resurrection of the body waits, Paul believes, in the not-too-distant future, he claims that those who trust in the Messiah have already experienced a movement from death to life, one that can be tracked via one's moral life, as the preceding chapter argued.

In other words, central to Paul's hopes and integral to his theology is the belief that the Messiah has been raised from the dead and that those in the Messiah will, after a short time, participate in the Messiah's resurrected state. Paul thinks that those who have died will not miss out and that both he and those who remain alive will also experience it. But what exactly is resurrection in Paul's thinking?

N. T. Wright has devoted a lengthy monograph to try to answer this question, suggesting that in Second Temple Judaism, resurrection *always* had to do with the reanimation and perfection of a person's flesh-and-blood body.[5] Consequently, he concludes that this is precisely what Paul must mean: the resurrection of those in the Messiah will be a resurrection of their flesh-and-blood bodies. Wright dismisses what he believes to be a gnostic view of resurrection that, he argues, wrongly reads Paul's thinking on resurrection in nonphysical ways: the disembodied soul persists after death, but there is no body. But there are several problems with Wright's argument.

One of the clearest and earliest texts about resurrection comes from the book of 2 Maccabees. The work depicts faithful Jews suffering at the hands of the foreign king Antiochus IV Epiphanes for their fidelity to the Jewish God and his laws. Seven sons and their mother undergo horrific torture but refuse to cave to the king's demands to break the Jewish law by eating pork (2 Macc. 7). After watching two of his brothers endure agonizing deaths, the third brother sticks out his hands and tongue to his torturers, saying, "I obtained these from heaven, and because of [God's] laws I despise them, and from him I hope to receive them again" (7:11). The fourth brother makes it clear that what motivates this pious family in the face of torture and death is their confidence that fidelity to God will result in God raising them from the dead (7:14).

The resurrection hope, then, is the belief in not only life after death but also embodied life, a body with holistic integrity. At least for the author of 2 Maccabees, resurrection has everything to do with the body. But it is less clear that the author necessarily must be thinking of a flesh-and-blood body. This is where we modern readers might unconsciously slip in an assumption that is foreign to ancient texts: the equation of the human body with flesh and blood. This might be justifiable in a text like 2 Maccabees, but then again, maybe not. The third brother says that if Antiochus IV takes away his limbs and tongue, he has every confidence that God will give them back to him at the resurrection. Does the author envisage the man receiving back the very hands and tongue that were cut off, or perhaps replacement

5. Wright, *Resurrection of the Son of God*.

limbs? How literal and how precise is the man's claim? And how literally should we take it? Could the man just mean that God will restore his bodily integrity without insisting on having *exactly* the same limbs that he had prior to his execution? And if this is possible, is it equally possible that resurrection from the dead means the restoration of a body that is not precisely the body with which one dies? These are not absurd questions. If someone is born without a limb, will their resurrected body have that limb? Or if someone loses a limb during their lifetime but then dies later, with which body will they be raised? If an infant dies, will that infant be raised as an infant or with a body of someone older? Will the person who dies at the age of one hundred receive back an aged body or a younger and stronger body?[6]

Modern science also impinges on this question. We know that our bodies are constantly changing. Most (not all, contrary to popular belief) of our body's cells replace themselves over a ten-year period. And the material that our bodies slough off over our lifetime gets incorporated into the bodies of other living beings. What is more, most of the cells within our bodies are not even humanoid.[7] How does one sensibly talk about the resurrection of the flesh-and-blood body in light of this modern knowledge? If one's flesh-and-blood body is raised from the dead, is it the same flesh one had before one died or new flesh and blood?

Ultimately, these modern questions are not all that different from ancient questions and knowledge about bodies. When Paul writes to Messiah followers in Corinth, he faces the same kinds of criticisms that some modern people have leveled against the Christian belief in resurrection. The key question that Paul addresses in 1 Corinthians 15:35–56 is what sort of body Messiah believers will have at the resurrection. We see this similar concern on the lips of one of Christianity's first detractors, the second-century philosopher Celsus, who, according to Origen, asked, "As for the flesh, which is full of things it is not even nice to mention, God would neither desire nor be able to

---

6. See Moss, *Divine Bodies*. In modern Christian theology, see Eiseland, *Disabled God*.
7. For one constructive attempt to deal with this reality, see Malcolm, "Body without End."

make it everlasting contrary to reason. . . . What sort of human soul would have any further desire for a body that has rotted?"[8] This is precisely the thinking among some in Corinth. Does one merely get back the body that one had at death? Well, that body has rotted, so who would want it back? And even if one got back a flesh-and-blood body free from rot, would it not still be subject to rot and decay and aging and, ultimately, death? If so, is such a resurrection *actually* good news? One need only consider the popular TV series *The Walking Dead*, which depicts a world in which the dead return to life as decaying zombies, to realize that returning from the dead is not always a good thing.

Paul is aware that he needs to show his readers that the resurrection he believes in is not one in which people receive back the very bodies they had when they died. To illustrate this fact, Paul turns to the scientific knowledge from his day. In the field of agriculture, one knows that what one puts in the dirt does not come out of the dirt: "And as for what you sow, you do not sow the body that is to be but a bare seed, perhaps of wheat or of some other grain. But God gives it a body as he has chosen and to each kind of seed its own body" (1 Cor. 15:37–38 NRSVue). The analogy suggests that Paul considers the flesh-and-blood body to be but a bare seed that dies and goes into the ground. Out of this simple kernel, a *new* body arises, a body that God chooses. As Nicholas Meyer puts it, "We expect . . . that when Paul begins to speak of the resurrection of the dead with the words 'it is sown . . . it is raised . . .' in v. 42 we will learn something of the contrasting *ontology* of the body before and after resurrection, in creation and recreation."[9]

Paul begins his discussion with the agricultural realm but then quickly shifts to the cosmological realm. Different seeds result in different types of bodies. Paul points to the diversity of animal life in the world: "There is one flesh for humans, another for animals, another for birds, and another for fish" (1 Cor. 15:39 NRSVue). Paul's

8. Origen, *Against Celsus* 5.14 (trans. Chadwick).
9. N. Meyer, *Adam's Dust and Adam's Glory*, 121–22.

taxonomy of animal flesh intentionally evokes taxonomies from Jewish scriptures. For instance, it runs in reverse order from the creation account of Genesis 1, which speaks of the creation of fish, birds, land animals, and finally humans (1:21, 25, 27). The distinctions God made at creation inform what the resurrection will be like as well. Had God made all bodies the same, animal life would not have been so varied and would not have been able to live in different habitats. Birds with fish flesh would not survive in the skies. Humans with fish flesh would be quite literally like fish out of water. To each ecosystem there is an appropriate and corresponding *flesh* body.

Paul's argument also evokes Psalm 8, a hymn that praises humanity's prime place in creation over land animals, birds, and fish (8:7–8). That this psalm is in Paul's mind is quite clear since earlier he quotes Psalm 8:6, depicting Israel's God placing all things under the resurrected Messiah's feet (1 Cor. 15:25–27).[10] It is this psalm that also speaks of God making humanity (and the Son of Man) lower than the gods (Hebrew: *elohim*) or the angels (LXX), an idea that Paul unpacks here in 1 Corinthians 15.

If earthly animals need different bodies suitable for each habitat, how much more necessary is it for heavenly beings to have different bodies suitable for a celestial ecosystem? And even in the celestial realm there are different bodies. At this point Paul makes a telling shift: he stops speaking of flesh (*sarx*) and begins to use the word "glory" (*doxa*). The implication is clear: terrestrial bodies (land, aquatic, avian) are fleshly bodies, but heavenly bodies are not. Even though the bodies of the sun, moon, and stars differ, they are all characterized as being bodies of *doxa*.

What many modern readers have failed to recognize is that Paul depends on a very common ancient cosmological belief that the sun, moon, and stars are living beings that have biological bodies. For instance, in his immensely influential cosmological book called the *Timaeus*, Plato provides the following taxonomy of living creatures:

10. The NRSVue unfortunately changes the singular "under his feet" in Ps. 8:6 (and other singular nouns and verbs) to "under their feet," hiding the messianic potential of the verse.

"And these Forms are four,—one the heavenly kind of gods [i.e., stars]; another winged kind which traverses the air; thirdly, the class which inhabits the waters; and fourthly, that which goes on foot on dry land." And he claims that the supreme God made the divine celestial animals "for the most part out of fire, that this kind might be as bright as possible to behold and as fair."[11] The language of bright-burning fire coincides with our modern popular understanding of the sun and stars (but not the moon) as fiery balls of gas. But one must not miss the fact that Plato thinks these are divine, living animals—lower divinities that populate the heavens.[12] This common understanding of celestial bodies as fiery brightness fits with Paul's use of the word *doxa* for the sun, moon, and stars, since many Jews thought of *doxa*, or the Hebrew word *kavod*, as something luminous. For instance, the book of Exodus describes how God descends to Mount Sinai in order to give the law to Moses in the following way: "Now the appearance of the glory [*kavod/doxa*] of Yhwh was like a devouring fire on the top of the mountain in the sight of the people of Israel" (24:17; cf. Deut. 5:24).[13]

Plato's thinking about the celestial bodies was shared by and likely influenced many Jews. Paul's Jewish contemporary Philo claims, "It seemed good to their Maker to fill all parts of the universe with living beings. He set land-animals on the earth, aquatic creatures in the seas and rivers, and in heaven the stars, each of which is said to be not a living creature only but mind of the purest kind through and through."[14] In other words, stars need a body suited to the environment of the realm in which they live. Such an environment is naturally hostile to flesh and blood. Neil Armstrong could not leave the safety of Apollo 11 in a tuxedo to celebrate being the first person to walk on the moon but had to wear a specially adapted suit (or body) to survive the moon's environment. So too ancient scientists knew that creatures needed to be properly embodied to dwell in heaven.

11. Plato, *Timaeus* 40A.

12. On the near ubiquity of this belief in the ancient world, see Scott, *Origen and the Life of the Stars*.

13. Other passages of Jewish scriptures that connect glory and radiance include Deut. 33:2; Isa. 10:16–17; Hab. 3:3–4; Pss. 84:11; 104:1–2.

14. Philo, *On Dreams* 1.135.

If we allow our own astrophysics to creep into our readings of 1 Corinthians 15, then we are bound to run into problems. Since most (perhaps all) of us make a sharp distinction between the material and spiritual realms, we might think that when Paul says "spiritual," he must mean nonphysical. Consider the NRSVue translation of 1 Corinthians 15:44, which distinguishes between the first body, which is sown, and the second body, which comes out of the sown seed: "It is sown a physical body; it is raised a spiritual body. If there is a physical body, there is also a spiritual body." There are at least two problems with this translation. First, the Greek word the translators render as "physical" is *psychikos*, a word that does not mean physical. Instead, it is related to the Greek word for soul—*psychē*. So while Paul is referring to a material body, that is not the point of the distinction he is making between the two bodies. Rather, he alludes to Genesis 2:7, which speaks of God making the earthling into a living soul (*eis psychēn zōsan*). In contrast to this original *psychikos* (soulish) body, the resurrection body will be a *pneumatic* body. Second, I prefer to use the term *pneumatic* rather than *spiritual* because it helps modern readers distance themselves from the assumption that what is spiritual is the opposite of material or physical. (Think, for example, of how often you hear that you must be grateful for your spiritual blessings rather than your material blessings.)

Paul does not use the ancient scientific language of *aether*, but when he speaks of the *doxa* of the heavenly bodies, it is clear he is talking about something quite similar. According to Aristotle, the material substance of the stars, *aether*, is divine, eternal, immutable, and incorruptible (*aphtharsia*). Aristotle goes on to associate *aether* with *pneuma*: "The nature which is in the *pneuma* . . . is analogous to the element of the stars [that is, *aether*]." In a work devoted to his understanding of *pneuma*, he makes it clear that *pneuma* is a body.[15] In Aristotle's thinking, *aether* functions in the celestial realm, but in the earthly realm it works through the vehicle of *pneuma*. Paul does not display this level of metaphysical sophistication in his discussion in 1 Corinthians 15,

---

15. Quotations of Aristotle come from *Generation of Animals* 2.736b38–2.737a1.

but he believes that God's *pneuma* acts in both the heavenly and the earthly realm.

Another problem with Wright's treatment of resurrection is his claim that non-Jewish Greeks and Romans universally rejected the idea of an embodied postmortem existence. Again, just because they (usually) reject the idea of a flesh-and-blood celestial existence does not mean they cannot think in terms of embodiment. One must take great care with claims about a disembodied soul. For many people the soul *was* a body. For instance, the Roman philosopher Seneca at times seems to suggest postmortem disembodiment, depicting the soul as saying, "When the day comes to separate the heavenly from its earthly blend, I shall leave the body here where I found it, and shall of my own volition betake myself to the gods." This sounds very much as though he believes the soul will be incorporeal after death. An even more detailed description of death might mislead modern readers as well: "You will be stripped of the very skin which covers you—that which has been your last protection; you will be stripped of the flesh, and lose the blood which is suffused and circulated through your body; you will be stripped of bones and sinews, the framework of these transitory and feeble parts."[16] But the stress is on the sort of body the soul leaves behind: "a heavy and earthly prison." In his consoling letter to Marcia, he states that after death souls "carry less weight of earthly dross."[17] Not *no* weight, just *less* weight. The flesh-and-blood body physically weighs down the soul so that it cannot ascend to heaven. Once the soul becomes *physically* detached from this anchor, it floats upward because it is light enough to do so. But it still has weight, much like a helium-filled balloon has weight and is a body, but one that is lighter than the surrounding air. And it is still a body, as he makes clear: "For the soul, too, is corporeal."[18]

Different bodies for different habitats. This is the consistent theme of ancient physics. The fifth-century BCE philosopher Anaxagoras argues that bodies take after the various elements of the universe and therefore dwell in places appropriate to those elements: "Some,

---

16. Seneca, *Moral Epistles* 102.22–23, 25.
17. Seneca, *To Marcia on Consolation* 23.1.
18. Seneca, *Moral Epistles* 106.5.

like earth, were heavy, occupying the region below, others, light like fire, held the region above, while water and air were intermediate in position."[19] What Anaxagoras implies here is that one element in particular, fire, is suited to a celestial realm. According to John Philoponus, the fourth-century BCE philosopher Heraclides of Pontus argued that the soul had a heavenly body (*ouranion sōma*).[20] This applied to the bodies of the gods, as Lucretius later makes clear: "Therefore, their [the gods'] abodes also must be different from our abodes, being thin in accord with their bodies."[21] Note that Lucretius takes it for granted that everyone will agree with him that gods have bodies and that such bodies are "thin"—not skinny, that is, but made of a very fine, light material. From this assumption, he argues that the abode of the gods must consist of a similar material.

This is, I believe, Paul's logic in a nutshell:

Living beings need to have the right body to dwell in a particular habitat.

The sun, stars, and moon are living beings.

As living beings, they must have the appropriate body for a celestial habitat.

This body is *not* a body of *sarx* (flesh) but a body of *doxa* (glory).

This *doxa*-body consists of the material of *pneuma*.

The Messiah had a flesh-and-blood body.

After his resurrection he became a *pneuma*.

There are two races of humanity:

Humanity according to the first Adam, characterized by *sarx*.

Humanity according to the last Adam (the Messiah), characterized by *pneuma*.

As Troels Engberg-Pedersen puts it, "Basically, then, Paul is relying on a single, straightforward contrast between an earthly kind of body

---

19. Diogenes Laertius, *Lives of Eminent Philosophers* 2.8.
20. John Philoponus, *Commentary on Aristotle's On the Soul* 1, prologue.
21. Lucretius, *On the Nature of Things* 5.153–154.

connected with death and a heavenly kind of body connected with
eternal life."[22] Let me stress again, Paul believes in the bodily resurrection of the dead. The dead will be raised with a body. Here Wright
is right. But this body will be a very different body from a flesh-and-
blood body. A seed goes into the ground, and a new body arises. The
first body, following the race of the first Adam, comes out of the dust
of the earth. It shares this dusty image with the first Adam. But such
a dirt body is constitutionally, ontologically inferior. It is made from
the lower elements, even as it is infused with God's breath.[23] The inferior material of earth is changeable, destructible, and mortal. Such
bodies age, deteriorate, decay, and die. They are made for a terrestrial
environment with all of its requirements and limitations. Who would
want such a body forever, and who would want such a body in a very
different environment? The last Adam, the Messiah, though he had
flesh and blood, *became* a life-giving *pneuma* after his resurrection. I
say *after* not *at* because I am not at all certain whether Paul thinks that
Jesus's resurrection *was* his transformation into a *pneuma* or whether
these were two separate events. Paul tells us nothing about an empty
tomb and gives us no detailed information about what was entailed
in Jesus's post-resurrection appearances to his followers (and then to
Paul himself). Does he think, like Luke, that the resurrected Jesus
had a flesh-and-blood body? This is quite plausible, since he continued to live in a terrestrial environment. If so, Jesus's transformation
into a life-giving *pneuma* must have occurred at his ascension to the
heavenly realm.

Paul's effort to show the intelligibility and attractiveness of his belief in the resurrection of the dead fundamentally depends on his use
of the common scientific beliefs of his day. Life in heaven requires
the right body, a body that heavenly beings already possess. Ancient
people had different names for these bodies, including *doxa*, *aether*,

22. Engberg-Pedersen, *Cosmology and Self*, 27.
23. This was a common Jewish view of the body based on Gen. 2. At Qumran the
Hodayot repeatedly stress how lowly humanity is precisely because it is made out of dirt,
while later rabbinic literature can point to this substance as the lowly animalistic aspect
of humanity (e.g., Genesis Rabbah 8.11).

and *pneuma*. Paul focuses primarily on *pneuma*, which has misled numerous people who do not share his scientific presuppositions. To their ears, *pneuma* is not material, not physical, not bodily. So either they make the mistake of concluding that Paul did not believe in a bodily resurrection, or they conclude that he did, thinking that the statement "the resurrection body is pneumatic" is a statement not about the type of body but about how the flesh-and-blood body is animated or empowered. In other words, the *pneuma* provides the flesh-and-blood body with immortality. Both conclusions are wrong and indebted to a different physics, which rose in popularity after Paul. Because of this change in science, early Christianity and much subsequent Christianity needed the resurrection body to be a (perfected) flesh-and-blood body.[24]

Paul believed in the bodily resurrection of the dead. This body did not consist of flesh and blood, inferior materials that have no place in the heavenly realms. It consisted, rather, of the material of *pneuma*. *Pneuma* is eternal, unchangeable, indestructible material. The. Best. Matter. Ever. We might disagree with Paul's physics (it would be odd for us not to, given the advances in science over the last two thousand years), but his claim that the resurrection body would be indestructible and eternal and immortal is something that Christianity has affirmed in different ways. In the Messiah's resurrection from the dead, "death has been swallowed up in victory" (1 Cor. 15:54). All that awaits is the final victory over death's forces and the resurrection of the entire race of the last Adam.

24. See Bynum, *Resurrection of the Body*. Bynum (26) connects the rise in the belief of the resurrection of the *flesh* to dogmatic battles within the nascent Christian movement: "Resurrection not of 'the dead' or 'the body' (*soma* or *corpus*) but of 'the flesh' (*sarx* or *caro*) became a key element in the fight against Docetism (which treated Christ's body as in some sense unreal or metaphorical) and Gnosticism (which carried 'realized eschatology' so far as to understand resurrection as spiritual and moral advance in this life and therefore as escape from body)."

12

The Messiah and the Jews

B
ut what about Paul's fellow Jews? Gentiles had to struggle with figuring out what bits of the Jewish law applied to them, but what bits of Paul's teachings and statements applied to his fellow Jews? If he wrote predominantly, if not exclusively, to non-Jews, what did any of this thinking have to do with Jews? Two possible answers to these questions ought to be avoided despite how attractive they might seem.

First, one could universalize Paul's statements so that they apply to all people, Jews and non-Jews, in precisely the same way. This has been a common approach to Paul's letters throughout the history of Christianity. But even a cursory reading of Paul's letters shows how impossible such a reading strategy is in general. For instance, no one reads Paul's letter to Philemon and concludes that one should have a guest room cleaned and tidy for Paul's imminent arrival (Philem. 22). And no one waits at the door for Onesimus to return in order to welcome him back (Philem. 12). These are obvious examples. Paul addresses certain letters to certain people in real situations that occurred in the past. His letters are full of context-specific instructions

and teachings that readers ever since have had to interpret both carefully and creatively to apply to their own lives. And, with regard to
ethnicity, I have already argued that in Romans 1:18–32 Paul does
not, contrary to the vast majority of modern interpreters, intend to
describe the sinful condition of all humanity. Rather, the passage
outlines the low points of the gentile condition: they rejected God,
descending into idolatry and from there into immorality. Almost all
ancient interpreters understood the ethnic specificity here and were
comfortable with it.

Second, one could conclude that none of what Paul wrote has relevance for Jews themselves. After all, Paul repeatedly claims that he
has been divinely ordained to bring the message of good news to
gentiles, not to Jews. To the Galatians, Paul claims that before he was
even born, Israel's God had set him apart to proclaim God's son to the
gentiles (1:16). And to the Romans, Paul claims that God gave him
grace and an ambassadorship to bring about the obedience of faith
among the gentiles (1:5). Paul repeats a similar claim twice more in
this letter (11:13; 15:16). And in Colossians and Ephesians, Paul or
his imitator claims to be a prisoner on behalf of the gentiles and that
God has commissioned him on their behalf (Col. 1:24–28; Eph. 3:1–2).
And another imitator of Paul continues this tradition, depicting Paul
as a herald, an envoy, and a teacher of the gentiles (1 Tim. 2:7), God's
vessel through whom gentiles hear the message (2 Tim. 4:17).[1] Consequently, some more recent interpreters have concluded that Paul
thinks that the good news of the Messiah pertains only to non-Jews.
Gentiles need to be saved by Jesus the Messiah; Jews do not. Such
a reading of Paul, often called the *Sonderweg* reading (German for
"special way"), was set forth in the English world most prominently
by Lloyd Gaston and John Gager and in the German world by Franz
Mussner.[2] These and other writers have proposed that there were two

1. Later Christian interpreters also stressed the ethnic-specific nature of Paul's man-
date: e.g., Acts 13:47; 1 Clement 5.7; Acts of Paul 11.3.
2. Gaston, *Paul and the Torah*, 33, 148; Gager, *Reinventing Paul*; and Mussner, "'Christus (ist) des Gesetzes Ende.'" See the related efforts of Boccaccini, *Paul's Three Paths to
Salvation.*

separate paths to salvation in Paul's mind. Paul thought that Jews ought to continue in their law-observant life without any need to believe in or follow Jesus. Gentiles, on the other hand, need the Messiah, which is why Paul traversed the Roman Empire to convince them that Jesus was the Messiah.

Many readers of Paul have found the *Sonderweg* reading to be historically implausible in light of what Paul writes in his letters. Given the centrality of the Messiah to Paul's thinking, could he really have believed that certain people would be saved apart from Jesus? Paul makes multiple claims that demonstrate that this reading, whatever its ecumenical value, is an inaccurate reading of Paul's own thinking. After all, in his letter to the Romans, which I have argued was written with gentile Messiah followers in mind and was addressed to them alone, Paul nonetheless proclaims that the good news (not *his* good news, mind you, which he talks about in Rom. 2:16 and 16:25) is God's power for the deliverance of Jews *first* and then for gentiles (1:16). And Paul insists that Jews too must become obedient to the good news through trust (10:14–16), the same obedience of faith he seeks to elicit among gentiles (1:5; 16:26). And to gentile Messiah followers in Galatia, Paul stresses that God has entrusted him with the task of bringing the message of the Messiah to the gentiles (literally, the foreskin), while this same God has entrusted Peter with being an envoy to the Jews (literally, the circumcision) (Gal. 2:7–9). Whatever the details of Peter's message to Jews were, surely they must have included something about Jesus being Israel's Messiah. What sense would it make for Israel's Messiah to have come only to be an irrelevant figure in the history and deliverance of his fellow Jews? The *Sonderweg* reading of Paul simply has not convinced most readers— and for good reason.

Traditional Christian theology frequently reads Paul as though one can provide from his writings some grand theory of what is wrong with Judaism as a religion. Especially since the Reformation, Christians have claimed that Paul abandoned Judaism because he came to see that it was a religion that required one to earn one's deliverance through good deeds and effort. Having come to see his own sinfulness,

Paul must have been driven to despair only to find that God wanted or expected people to be saved not by their own righteousness but by trusting the Messiah. Those Jews who did not believe in Jesus had a misplaced confidence or arrogance in their own ability to please and obey God. This remains a common reading of Paul, but it better describes Martin Luther's own life story. After all, Paul makes no claims about how sinful, hopeless, and full of despair he was prior to becoming a follower of Jesus. Instead, in the few places Paul describes his pre-messianic experience, he does so in rather glowing terms. He was advancing in "Judaism" far beyond his peers when God abruptly interrupted his life to make him the herald to the gentiles (Gal. 1:14–15). And, no doubt to Luther's chagrin, Paul even boasts that with regard to righteousness in relation to the law, he was blameless (*amemptos*) (Phil. 3:6), the exact same language that gets used of Job (Job 1:1, 8; 2:3) and the state of being to which God calls Abraham (Gen. 17:1).

And since E. P. Sanders's 1977 paradigm-shifting *Paul and Palestinian Judaism*, scholars have largely realized that describing ancient Judaism as a religion of works righteousness is not an accurate historical description but a theological apologetic that uses Judaism as a foil for Christianity. As John Barclay has recently reconfirmed, "Grace is everywhere in Second Temple Judaism but not everywhere the same. . . . Paul stands in the midst of this diversity. His theology of grace does not stand in antithesis to Judaism, but neither is there a common Jewish view with which it wholly coincides."[3]

The most difficult passage to reconcile with the claim that Paul found nothing wrong with Judaism is found in Romans 11. Here, to many readers, Paul seems to contrast Jewish works and Christian grace: "But if it is by grace, then it is no longer out of works, since grace would no longer be grace" (11:6). I should stress that this statement has the potential to be problematic for all readings of Paul. Does Paul here suggest that God had formerly delivered people on the basis of their works but now is choosing to be gracious? That would be a dramatic change to God's economy and character, reeking of an

---

3. Barclay, *Paul and the Gift*, 6.

odious supersessionism that contrasts the mean Old Testament God to the loving New Testament God. And does Paul really claim that in Elijah's day some people were saved by works—something he rejects repeatedly (e.g., Rom. 3:20; Gal. 2:16)? If people could be delivered through their actions, what need would they have of the Messiah (Gal. 2:21)?

This cannot be Paul's meaning, and the context helps clarify the point he seeks to make. Remember that the entirety of Romans 9–11 functions to explain why so few Jews have become convinced that Jesus is the Messiah and that Israel's God has raised him from the dead. Paul reminds his readers that God has not rejected his people, as shown by the fact that some Jews do believe in Jesus. And Israel's history provides a precedent for the current crisis: in the days of Elijah many of God's people had turned to worship Baal. But even then, there was a remnant of faithful Israelites who had not turned from God: *God had kept for himself* seven thousand who had not worshiped Baal. The idea of a loyal remnant precedes Paul, but Paul employs it here to explain the current situation. The faithful remnant in Elijah's day was distinguished by works: the work of loyally worshiping Israel's God and not Baal. In contrast, the remnant of Israel in Paul's day is not distinguished by fidelity to Israel's God in contrast to others who have handed themselves over to idolatry. After all, most Jews in Paul's day sought to keep faith with their God and rejected worship of other gods. This new remnant could not be distinguished this way, then. Further, its existence was dependent on God's grace—this remnant has come into existence only because God has chosen it to do so. It is identifiable by this grace and this trust in Jesus. But what, then, does Paul think the problem is for Jews who are not part of this remnant?

If all Jews believed in God's grace, even as they perhaps emphasized different aspects of that grace, from its priority to its efficacy to its incongruity, then Judaism cannot be described as a religion of works righteousness. If Jews believed in grace, were they already good "Protestants" with whom Paul had no problem? In the wake of Sanders's work, James Dunn and N. T. Wright both redescribed

Judaism in terms of another fatal flaw: OK, Jews weren't legalistic people seeking to earn their way into heaven; rather, and perhaps worse, they were ethnocentric people who stressed "race, not grace."[4] Again, such descriptions of Judaism depict it in ways that fail to do it justice.

Since Paul repeatedly describes himself as an envoy to the gentiles, and since his letters repeatedly stress the gentile identity of his intended readers, one must be careful not to take statements he makes about gentiles and wrongly apply them to Jews. How fortunate for the question of this chapter, then, that Paul has left a distilled statement about his fellow Jews in Romans 9–11.

Writing to non-Jews in Rome, Paul exclaims that he wishes that he were cut off from the Messiah for the sake of his fellow Jews (Rom. 9:3). Incidentally, these three chapters provide strong evidence that Paul does not envisage himself writing to Jewish believers or even a mixed audience of Jewish and gentile believers. One can see this already in Romans 9:4, where Paul speaks about his fellow Jews in the third person ("they," "to them," etc.). The fact that Paul wishes himself cut off from the Messiah for their sake demonstrates the seriousness of the predicament he believes them to be in. And yet immediately after this dramatic beginning, Paul rehearses the benefits that *still* belong to Jews: "They are Israelites. To them is the adoption and the glory and the covenants and the giving of the law and the temple service and the promises. To them are the ancestors and from out of them is the Messiah according to the flesh" (9:4–5).[5]

Such claims sound like Paul is committed to the very "ethnocentrism" of which Dunn and Wright accuse early Judaism. Jews remain God's adopted. God's covenants and gifts of his glory and the law and the temple and his promises remain their possessions. But while the

---

4. Such is the implication of N. T. Wright's claim (*Climax of the Covenant*, 194, 247) that Paul differs from Judaism in preaching "grace, not race."

5. To say as does Ambrosiaster (*Commentary on Romans* 9:4) that "by not accepting the Savior [Jews] lose the privilege of their fathers and the merit of the promises, and they became worse than the Gentiles" is to deny precisely what Paul still believes to be true. Unfortunately, most Christians have followed the thinking of Ambrosiaster and not Paul here.

Messiah has descended from them, many Jews, to Paul's surprise and consternation, have not recognized Jesus as their Messiah.

Paul's only accusation against his fellow Jews who do not believe that Jesus is Israel's Messiah is just that: they do not believe that Jesus is Israel's Messiah. This accusation has nothing to do with some abstract theory of works righteousness or legalism or ethnocentrism. They have stumbled over none of these things. Instead, Paul argues, quoting scripture, they have "stumbled over the stumbling stone" (Rom. 9:33; cf. Isa. 8:14; 28:16). Paul declares to his gentile readers that his fellow Jews are rightly zealous for God but that many of them remain unaware of the justice or righteousness of God (10:3). This righteousness and this stumbling stone are nothing other than the Messiah himself, who is the *telos*, or culmination, of the law (10:4). Paul believes that many Jews have failed to reach the goal of the law because of their very focus on the law. To use an analogy, this situation is like the person who is so engrossed in discerning the details of a map that they fail to make the final turn to get to their destination. This is Paul's assessment of the current situation.

This might sound like a criticism of Jews who do not recognize Jesus to be the Messiah or a criticism of the law, but Paul is relatively circumspect here. In Romans 11 he bends over backward to provide an explanation for this stunning end-time situation in which the Messiah's arrival goes unrecognized by many of his fellow Jews. Some Jews were convinced that Jesus was the Messiah, and Paul points to himself as one key example. But Paul does not demonize or even castigate other Jews who do not believe. Rather, he claims that Israel's *God* has hardened other Jews so that they would not perceive Jesus to be the Messiah. God gave them eyes with which they could not see and ears with which they could not hear (Rom. 11:8, again depending on scripture: Isa. 29:10). Why did God do this? It was through the stumbling of unbelief in the Messiah that God's deliverance could be extended to the gentile world (11:11–12). The Jews' rejection of the good news of the Messiah has allowed the cosmos to undergo reconciliation (11:15). This divine hardening of many Jews, Paul is convinced, is a temporary situation, one that serendipitously results in gentiles receiving deliverance (11:25). It is not permanent. It is not the final word, because God has elected Israel for the sake of their ancestors. And God's call and God's election cannot be undone. There are no take-backs on the gifts God gives (11:28 29).

What all of Romans 9–11 suggests is that there was and is nothing wrong with "Judaism" in Paul's mind. What has happened to many (but not all) of his fellow Jews is that God has mysteriously and temporarily hardened them so that they will not recognize their Messiah. This was done not in divine judgment but in order that God's delivering and reconciling work might be extended to all humanity. It would be bitterly ironic, then, were God's hardening of Israel on behalf of non-Jews to result in gentiles being saved to the near exclusion of all Jews. For Paul, such a thought was impossible. God would never reject his people, even if they failed to recognize the coming of the Messiah. Just as God has had mercy on the gentiles who are now streaming into the Jesus movement, so he should have mercy on the Jews whom he has temporarily caused to disbelieve. God will be merciful to all.

Romans 11:28–32 presents in a nutshell, then, what Paul thinks is wrong with Judaism. Despite all the many failings of Israel that ancient Jewish writers unflinchingly depict from Genesis to Paul's day, Paul does not emphasize these historical failings of idolatry and so on. Instead, Paul's history of Israel implies that, whatever sins Jews have committed, they were still God's people. Paul can categorize Jews, unlike the gentiles, as formerly obedient. Only in the messianic *now* has the majority of Israel found itself cut off. And this current disobedience is divinely ordained and orchestrated with the intention that God would not permit this state to continue. He will remove this hardening at some future point, having mercy on gentiles and Jews alike.

For modern ecumenical discussions, this might not be what some desire. It would be more convenient, perhaps, were Paul to have claimed that Jews did not need to believe that Jesus was the Messiah. And it certainly would be more convenient had he not claimed that God had temporarily hardened many of his fellow Jews. But Romans

9–11 represents Paul's best effort to reconcile his conviction that the Messiah had indeed come with the odd fact that many Jews in his day did not recognize the Messiah's coming. For Paul, this hardening would be temporary and short lived. Were Paul to be conjured two thousand or so years later, would he still hold to this view, or would he need to revise his thinking?

Conclusion

P aul found nothing wrong with Judaism. In his mind, there was nothing deficient with it. Contrary to the anti-legalistic reading, Paul did not think Judaism was a religion that required people to earn their salvation. Contrary to the anti-ethnocentric reading, neither did Paul think Judaism led to ethnic pride and racial exclusion. The key to unlocking Paul's writings is to embed him within the larger Jewish world of his day. His many statements about the Jewish law and circumcision must be understood within Jewish debates about how non-Jews are supposed to relate to Israel's God, Israel, and Israel's law. Such debates and disagreements were common and ongoing among ancient Jews, and Paul and others who believed that Jesus was the Messiah continued to debate and disagree over the place of non-Jews. This debate became especially heated in a movement that began to attract an ever-growing number of non-Jews into what was initially just one more Jewish way of life.

To construct ancient Judaism as a legalistic religion, or as a religion that required one to earn God's favor, or as a religion that was ethnocentric and exclusivist is overly simplified and historically inaccurate. And it should not need saying, but if Christians feel they must make Judaism (or other religions) look bad and must mischaracterize them to make Christianity appealing to themselves and others, this does not bode well for the Christian faith. Think of a relationship in which one friend feels like they must constantly insult others for their friend to continue to like them. Such behavior is unfortunate, immature, and ultimately self-defeating.

I have sought in this small book to introduce people to a way of reading Paul that does not make Judaism into a foil for Christianity and that does not denigrate Jews, the Jewish law, or Judaism to make Paul appear like a hero. Paul was convinced that in the Messiah's incarnation, death, and resurrection gentiles were being incorporated into God's eschatological deliverance. His message was a message of inclusion for those who believed that Jesus was the Messiah and that Israel's God had raised him from the dead. God's delivering action was related to his various promises to Abraham and to Abraham's seed. To get access to these many promises, gentiles needed to somehow become related to Abraham. This belief was no less ethnocentric than the beliefs of other Jews (both those who believed that Jesus was the Messiah and those who did not). Some gentiles became convinced that the way to connect to Abraham was via the rite of circumcision and the subsequent observance of the Jewish law. For Paul, this put an absurd amount of confidence in works of the law to transform gentiles into Abrahamic seed. Gentile circumcision was nothing more than cosmetic surgery that gave gentiles the appearance of belonging to Abraham without the substance of belonging to Abraham. Worse yet, by placing confidence in such deeds, gentiles were also implying (probably unintentionally) that the Messiah and the Messiah's *pneuma* had not effectively connected them to Abraham. For Paul, a divine act of pneumatic infusion had resulted in forging a real connection to Abraham. Out of nothing, out of no genealogical relation, God created something new: flesh-and-blood gentiles who now possess the Messiah's *pneuma* and who are therefore both Abraham's sons and God's sons. Israel, Israel's ancestors, and Abrahamic descent continued to matter for Paul, even as he focused on non-Jews.

Now being connected to Abraham, gentiles who are loyal to Jesus the Messiah are infused with a new moral power so that they can live holy lives that reflect the shape of the Messiah's life. They are morally revivified to continue bearing the Messiah's presence to the world.

They do this as they await the final resurrection, where they will be fully divinized and rule with the Messiah forever.

"There are some things in them hard to understand, which the ignorant and unstable twist to their own destruction" (2 Pet. 3:16 NRSVue). That might be a disturbing acknowledgment about Paul's letters, especially for someone who has just finished writing a short book on Paul, but I choose to read it as liberating. Do I understand every statement or every passage in Paul's letters? I do not. Many passages I do not fully comprehend or know how, or if, they fit within my overall understanding of Paul's thinking. Paul's writings do not lend themselves to easy or perfect categorization. And his writings have been hard to understand since the moment they were written. It is liberating to know that I am not alone in continuing to wrestle and struggle with Paul, seeking to provide a coherent account of his thought based on his unruly and fragmentary literary remains.

It is common for biblical scholars to respond to each other with various *what abouts*—what about this or that passage, as though such a question necessarily undoes the claims of one's arguments. I imagine many readers have asked that very question more than once while reading through this book. What about this or that text or statement? I have frequently fought off the temptation to try to anticipate such *what abouts* in this book, reminding myself that I am merely *introducing* readers to a particular approach to Paul, not providing a definitive defense of it. Rather, my hope is that the questions, the concerns, the *what abouts* some of you might have asked as you read this little book might spur you on to think through Paul's letters in light of an approach that seeks to defuse Christian anti-Judaism and supersessionism.

Bibliography

Allison, Dale. *The Resurrection of Jesus: Apologetics, Polemics, History*. London: T&T Clark, 2021.

Ambrosiaster. *Commentaries on Romans and 1–2 Corinthians*. Translated and edited by Gerald L. Bray. Ancient Christian Texts. Downers Grove, IL: IVP Academic, 2009.

Athanasius. *Contra Gentes and De Incarnatione* [Against the pagans and on the incarnation]. Edited and translated by Robert W. Thomson. Oxford Early Christian Texts. Oxford: Clarendon, 1971.

Augustine. *Augustine on Romans: Propositions from the Epistle to the Romans, Unfinished Commentary on the Epistle to the Romans*. Translated by Paula Fredriksen Landes. Society of Biblical Literature Texts and Translations 23. Chico, CA: Scholars Press, 1982.

Aune, David. "Mastery of the Passions: Philo, 4 Maccabees and Earliest Christianity." Pages 125–58 in *Hellenization Revisited: Shaping a Christian Response within the Greco-Roman World*. Edited by Wendy E. Helleman. Lanham, MD: University Press of America, 1994.

Barclay, John M. G. *Paul and the Gift*. Grand Rapids: Eerdmans, 2015.

Baron, Lori, Jill Hicks-Keeton, and Matthew Thiessen, eds. *The Ways That Often Parted: Essays in Honor of Joel Marcus*. Early Christian Literature 24. Atlanta: SBL Press, 2018.

Barth, Karl. *Church Dogmatics*. 4 vols. Edinburgh: T&T Clark, 1956–75.

Bauckham, Richard. *Jesus and the God of Israel: God Crucified and Other Studies on the New Testament's Christology of Divine Identity*. Grand Rapids: Eerdmans, 2008.

Bauckham, Richard, James R. Davila, and Alexander Panayotov, eds. *Old Testament Pseudepigrapha: More Noncanonical Scriptures*. Grand Rapids: Eerdmans, 2013.

Bazzana, Giovanni B. *Having the Spirit of Christ: Spirit Possession and Exorcism in the Early Christ Groups*. Synkrisis. New Haven: Yale University Press, 2019.

Becker, Adam, and Annette Yoshiko Reed, eds. *The Ways That Never Parted: Jews and Christians in Late Antiquity and the Early Middle Ages*. Minneapolis: Fortress, 2007.

Berlin, Anne Deborah. "Shame of the Gentiles of Profiat Duran: A Fourteenth-Century Jewish Polemic against Christianity." BA thesis, Harvard University, 1987.

Boakye, Andrew. *Death and Life: Resurrection, Restoration, and Rectification in Paul's Letter to the Galatians*. Eugene, OR: Wipf & Stock, 2017.

Boccaccini, Gabriele. *Paul's Three Paths to Salvation*. Grand Rapids: Eerdmans, 2020.

Bos, Abraham P. *Aristotle on God's Life-Generating Power and on the* Pneuma *as Its Vehicle*. Albany, NY: SUNY, 2018.

Bos, Abraham P., and Rein Ferwerda. *Aristotle, On the Life-Bearing Spirit (*De Spiritu*): A Discussion with Plato and His Predecessors on* Pneuma *as the Instrumental Body of the Soul*. Leiden: Brill, 2008.

Bowens, Lisa. *African American Readings of Paul: Reception, Resistance, and Transformation*. Grand Rapids: Eerdmans, 2020.

Boyarin, Daniel. *A Radical Jew: Paul and the Politics of Identity*. Berkeley: University of California Press, 1997.

Brand, Miryam T. *Evil Within and Without: The Source of Sin and Its Nature as Portrayed in Second Temple Literature*. Journal of Ancient Judaism Supplements 9. Göttingen: Vandenhoeck & Ruprecht, 2013.

Braude, William G. *The Midrash on Psalms*. 2 vols. Yale Judaica Series 13. New Haven: Yale University Press, 1959.

Bynum, Caroline Walker. *The Resurrection of the Body in Western Christianity, 200–1336*. Lectures on the History of Religions 15. New York: Columbia University Press, 1995.

Campbell, Douglas. *The Deliverance of God: An Apocalyptic Rereading of Justification in Paul*. Grand Rapids: Eerdmans, 2009.

———. "Galatians 5.11: Evidence of an Early Law Observant Mission by Paul." *New Testament Studies* 57 (2011): 325–47.

———. "The Story of Jesus in Romans and Galatians." Pages 97–124 in *Narrative Dynamics in Paul: A Critical Assessment*. Edited by Bruce W. Longenecker. Louisville: Westminster John Knox, 2002.

Campbell, William. *Unity and Diversity in Christ: Interpreting Paul in Context; Collected Essays*. Eugene, OR: Cascade Books, 2013.

Charles, Ronald. *Paul and the Politics of Diaspora*. Minneapolis: Fortress, 2014.

Charlesworth, James H., ed. *The Old Testament Pseudepigrapha*. 2 vols. Garden City, NY: Doubleday, 1983–85.

Chin, C. M. "Marvelous Things Heard: On Finding Historical Radiance." *Massachusetts Review* 58 (2017): 478–91.

Cohen, Shaye J. D. "Respect for Judaism by Gentiles according to Josephus." *Harvard Theological Review* 80 (1987): 409–30.

Cohn-Sherbok, Dan. *Messianic Judaism*. London: Cassell, 2000.

Collman, Ryan. *The Apostle to the Foreskin: Circumcision in the Letters of Paul.* Beihefte zur Zeitschrift für die neutestamentliche Wissenschaft 259. Berlin: de Gruyter, 2023.

Cook, John Granger. *Crucifixion in the Mediterranean World*. 2nd ed. Wissenschaftliche Untersuchungen zum Neuen Testament 327. Tübingen: Mohr Siebeck, 2019.

de Bruyn, Theodore. *Pelagius' Commentary on St Paul's Epistle to the Romans: Translated with Introduction and Notes*. Oxford Early Christian Studies. Oxford: Clarendon, 1993.

Donaldson, Terence L. *Gentile Christian Identity from Cornelius to Constantine: The Nations, the Parting of the Ways, and Roman Imperial Ideology*. Grand Rapids: Eerdmans, 2020.

———. *Judaism and the Gentiles: Jewish Patterns of Universalism (to 135 CE)*. Waco: Baylor University Press, 2007.

Dunn, James D. G. "The New Perspective on Paul." *Bulletin of the John Ryland's Library* 65 (1983): 95–122.

———. *The New Perspective on Paul*. Rev. ed. Grand Rapids: Eerdmans, 2008.

———. *The Theology of Paul the Apostle*. Grand Rapids: Eerdmans, 1997.

Eco, Umberto. "The Theory of Signs and the Role of the Reader." *Bulletin of the Midwest Modern Language Association* 14 (1981): 35–45.

Ehrensperger, Kathy. *Searching Paul: Conversations with the Jewish Apostle to the Nations*. Wissenschaftliche Untersuchungen zum Neuen Testament 429. Tübingen: Mohr Siebeck, 2019.

Ehrman, Bart. *Forgery and Counterforgery: The Use of Literary Deceit in Early Christian Polemics*. New York: Oxford University Press, 2012.

Eiseland, Nancy. *The Disabled God: Toward a Liberatory Theology of Disability*. Nashville: Abingdon, 1994.

Eisenbaum, Pamela. *Paul Was Not a Christian: The Original Message of a Misunderstood Apostle*. New York: HarperOne, 2009.

Engberg-Pedersen, Troels. *Cosmology and Self in the Apostle Paul: The Material Spirit*. Oxford: Oxford University Press, 2010.

———, ed. *Paul Beyond the Judaism/Hellenism Divide*. Louisville: Westminster John Knox, 2001.

———, ed. *Paul in His Hellenistic Context*. Minneapolis: Augsburg Fortress, 1995.

Eyl, Jennifer. "'I Myself Am an Israelite': Paul, Authenticity and Authority." *Journal for the Study of the New Testament* 40 (2017): 148–68.

———. "Semantic Voids, New Testament Translation, and Anachronism: The Case of Paul's Use of *Ekklēsia*." *Method and Theory in the Study of Religion* 26 (2014): 315–39.

Fitzgerald, John T., ed. *Passions and Moral Progress in Greco-Roman Thought.* Routledge Monographs in Classical Studies. New York: Routledge, 2008.

Fletcher-Louis, Crispin. "'The Being That Is in a Manner Equal with God' (Phil. 2:6c): A Self-Transforming, Incarnational, Divine Ontology." *Journal of Theological Studies* 71 (2020): 581–627.

Fredriksen, Paula. "*Al Tirah* ('Fear Not!'): Jewish Apocalyptic Eschatology, from Schweitzer to Allison, and After." Pages 15–38 in *"To Recover What Has Been Lost": Essays on Eschatology, Intertextuality, and Reception History in Honor of Dale C. Allison Jr.* Edited by Tucker Ferda, Daniel Frayer-Griggs, and Nathan C. Johnson. Supplements to Novum Testamentum 183. Leiden: Brill, 2021.

———. "Judaism, the Circumcision of Gentiles, and Apocalyptic Hope: Another Look at Galatians 1–2." *Journal of Theological Studies* 42 (1991): 532–64.

———. *Paul: The Pagans' Apostle.* New Haven: Yale University Press, 2017.

———. "Philo, Herod, Paul, and the Many Gods of Ancient Jewish 'Monotheism.'" *Harvard Theological Review* 115 (2022): 23–45.

———. *Sin: The Early History of an Idea.* Princeton: Princeton University Press, 2012.

Gaca, Kathy. "Paul's Uncommon Declaration in Romans 1:18–32 and Its Problematic Legacy for Pagan and Christian Relations." *Harvard Theological Review* 92 (1999): 165–98.

Gaddis, John Lewis. *The Landscape of History: How Historians Map the Past.* Oxford: Oxford University Press, 2002.

Gager, John. *Reinventing Paul.* Oxford: Oxford University Press, 2000.

Gallagher, Edmon L., and John D. Meade. *The Biblical Canon Lists in Early Christianity: Texts and Analysis.* Oxford: Oxford University Press, 2017.

Garroway, Joshua. *The Beginning of the Gospel: Paul, Philippi, and the Origins of Christianity.* New York: Palgrave Macmillan, 2018.

Gaston, Lloyd. *Paul and the Torah.* Vancouver: University of British Columbia Press, 1987.

Gilliard, Frank. "The Problem of the Antisemitic Comma between 1 Thessalonians 2.14 and 15." *New Testament Studies* 35 (1989): 481–502.

Gil-White, Francisco J. "How Thin Is Blood? The Plot Thickens: If Ethnic Actors Are Primordialists, What Remains of the Circumstantialist/Primordialist Controversy?" *Ethnic and Racial Studies* 22 (1999): 789–820.

Goodman, Martin. *Mission and Conversion: Proselytizing in the Religious History of the Roman Empire.* Oxford: Clarendon, 1994.

Gupta, Nijay. "To Whom Was Christ a Slave (Phil 2:7)? Double Agency and the Specters of Sin and Death in Philippians." *Horizons in Biblical Theology* 32 (2010): 1–16.

Harrington, Hannah K. *The Purity and Sanctuary of the Body in Second Temple Judaism.* Journal of Ancient Judaism Supplement 33. Göttingen: Vandenhoeck & Ruprecht, 2019.

Hart, David Bentley. *That All Shall Be Saved: Heaven, Hell, and Universal Salvation.* New Haven: Yale University Press, 2019.

Hayes, Christine. "The Complicated Goy in Classical Rabbinic Sources." Pages 147–67 in *Perceiving the Other in Ancient Judaism and Early Christianity.* Edited by Michal Bar-Asher Siegal, Wolfgang Grünstäudl, and Matthew Thiessen. Wissenschaftliche Untersuchungen zum Neuen Testament 394. Tübingen: Mohr Siebeck, 2017.

———. *What's Divine about Divine Law? Early Perspectives.* Princeton: Princeton University Press, 2015.

Heim, Turid Karlsen. "In Heaven as on Earth? Resurrection, Body, Gender and Heavenly Rehearsals in Luke-Acts." Pages 17–42 in *Christian and Islamic Gender Models in Formative Traditions.* Edited by Kari Elisabeth Børresen. Rome: Herder, 2004.

Hengel, Martin. *Crucifixion in the Ancient World and the Folly of the Message of the Cross.* Translated by John Bowden. Philadelphia: Fortress, 1977.

Hengel, Martin, and Anna Maria Schwemer. *Paul between Damascus and Antioch: The Unknown Paul.* Translated by John Bowden. Louisville: Westminster John Knox, 1997.

Hewitt, J. Thomas. *Messiah and Scripture: Paul's "In Christ" Idiom in Its Ancient Jewish Context.* Wissenschaftliche Untersuchungen zum Neuen Testament 2/522. Tübingen: Mohr Siebeck, 2020.

Hodge, Caroline Johnson. *If Sons, Then Heirs: A Study of Kinship and Ethnicity in the Letters of Paul.* New York: Oxford University Press, 2007.

Horrell, David. *Ethnicity and Inclusion: Religion, Race, and Whiteness in Constructions of Jewish and Christian Identities.* Grand Rapids: Eerdmans, 2020.

Hurtado, Larry. *One God, One Lord: Early Christian Devotion and Ancient Jewish Monotheism.* 3rd ed. London: T&T Clark, 2015.

Isaac, Benjamin. *The Invention of Racism in Classical Antiquity.* Princeton: Princeton University Press, 2002.

Jewett, Robert. "Romans as an Ambassadorial Letter." *Interpretation* 36 (1982): 5–20.

Jipp, Joshua. *Christ Is King: Paul's Royal Ideology.* Minneapolis: Fortress, 2015.

———. *The Messianic Theology of the New Testament.* Grand Rapids: Eerdmans, 2020.

John Chrysostom. *Homilies on the Acts of the Apostles and the Epistle to the Romans*. Vol. 11 of *The Nicene and Post-Nicene Fathers*, Series 1. Edited by Philip Schaff. 1886–89. 14 vols. Reprint, Peabody, MA: Hendrickson, 1994.

Käsemann, Ernst. "The Beginnings of Christian Theology." Pages 82–107 in *New Testament Questions of Today*. Translated by W. J. Montague. Philadelphia: Fortress, 1969.

Kennedy, Rebecca F., C. Sydnor Roy, and Max L. Goldman, eds. *Race and Ethnicity in the Classical World: An Anthology of Primary Sources in Translation*. Indianapolis: Hackett, 2013.

Kim, Seyoon. *The Origins of Paul's Gospel*. Wissenschaftliche Untersuchungen zum Neuen Testament 2/4. Tübingen: Mohr Siebeck, 1984.

———. "Paul as an Eschatological Herald." Pages 9–24 in *Paul as Missionary: Identity, Activity, Theology, and Practice*. Edited by Trevor J. Burke and Brian S. Rosner. Library of New Testament Studies 420. London: T&T Clark, 2011.

Kinzer, Mark. *Postmissionary Messianic Judaism: Redefining Christian Engagement with the Jewish People*. Grand Rapids: Brazos, 2015.

Kirk, J. R. Daniel. *Unlocking Romans: Resurrection and the Justification of God*. Grand Rapids: Eerdmans, 2008.

Klawans, Jonathan. *Josephus and the Theologies of Ancient Judaism*. Oxford: Oxford University Press, 2012.

Kloppenborg, John S. *Christ's Associations: Connecting and Belonging in the Ancient City*. New Haven: Yale University Press, 2019.

Korner, Ralph. *The Origin and Meaning of* Ekklēsia *in the Early Jesus Movement*. Ancient Judaism and Early Christianity 98. Leiden: Brill, 2017.

Kotrosits, Maia. *The Lives of Objects: Material Culture, Experience, and the Real in the History of Early Christianity*. Chicago: University of Chicago Press, 2020.

Langton, Daniel R. *The Apostle Paul in the Jewish Imagination: A Study in Modern Jewish-Christian Relations*. Cambridge: Cambridge University Press, 2010.

Lee, Max. *Moral Transformation in Greco-Roman Philosophy of Mind: Mapping the Moral Milieu of the Apostle Paul and His Diaspora Jewish Contemporaries*. Wissenschaftliche Untersuchungen zum Neuen Testament 2/515. Tübingen: Mohr Siebeck, 2020.

Lee, Michelle V. *Paul, the Stoics, and the Body of Christ*. Society for New Testament Studies Monograph Series 137. Cambridge: Cambridge University Press, 2006.

Litwa, M. David. *Iesus Deus: The Early Christian Depiction of Jesus as a Mediterranean God*. Minneapolis: Fortress, 2013.

Long, A. G., ed. *Immortality in Ancient Philosophy*. Cambridge: Cambridge University Press, 2021.

Lopez, Davina C. *Apostle to the Conquered: Reimagining Paul's Mission*. Paul in Critical Contexts. Minneapolis: Fortress, 2010.

Luther, Martin. *The Bondage of the Will.* Pages 158–258 in vol. 2 of *The Annotated Luther.* Edited by Hans J. Hillerbrand, Kirsi I. Stjerna, and Timothy J. Wengert. 6 vols. Minneapolis: Fortress, 2015–17.

Malcolm, Hannah. "Body without End: Biological Mutualism and the Body of Christ." *International Journal of Systematic Theology* (2022): 1–17.

Marcus, Joel. "The Circumcision and the Uncircumcision in Rome." *New Testament Studies* 35 (1989): 67–81.

Martyn, J. Louis. *Galatians: A New Translation with Introduction and Commentary.* Anchor Bible 33A. New York: Doubleday, 1997.

———. *Theological Issues in the Letters of Paul.* Nashville: Abingdon, 1997.

Masuzawa, Tomoko. *The Invention of World Religions: Or, How European Universalism Was Preserved in the Language of Pluralism.* Chicago: University of Chicago Press, 2005.

McCaulley, Esau. *Sharing in the Son's Inheritance: Davidic Messianism and Paul's Worldwide Interpretation of the Abrahamic Land Promise in Galatians.* Library of New Testament Studies 608. London: T&T Clark, 2019.

McKnight, Scot, and B. J. Oropeza, eds. *Perspectives on Paul: Five Views.* Grand Rapids: Baker Academic, 2020.

Meyer, Anthony. *Naming God in Early Judaism: Aramaic, Hebrew, and Greek.* Studies in Cultural Contexts of the Bible 2. Leiden: Brill, 2022.

Meyer, Nicholas. *Adam's Dust and Adam's Glory in the Hodayot and the Letters of Paul: Rethinking Anthropogony and Theology.* Supplements to Novum Testamentum 168. Leiden: Brill, 2016.

Milgrom, Jacob. "The Dynamics of Purity in the Priestly System." Pages 29–32 in *Purity and Holiness: The Heritage of Leviticus.* Edited by Marcel J. H. M. Poorthuis and Joshua Schwartz. Jewish and Christian Perspectives Series 2. Leiden: Brill, 2000.

Mitchell, Margaret M. *The Heavenly Trumpet: John Chrysostom and the Art of Pauline Interpretation.* Louisville: Westminster John Knox, 2002.

Moffitt, David. *Rethinking the Atonement: New Perspectives on Jesus's Death, Resurrection, and Ascension.* Grand Rapids: Baker Academic, 2022.

Morgan, Teresa. *Being "in Christ" in the Letters of Paul: Saved through Christ and in His Hands.* Wissenschaftliche Untersuchungen zum Neuen Testament 449. Tübingen: Mohr Siebeck, 2020.

———. *Roman Faith and Christian Faith:* Pistis *and* Fides *in the Early Roman Empire and Early Churches.* Oxford: Oxford University Press, 2015.

Moss, Candida. *Divine Bodies: Resurrecting Perfection in the New Testament and Early Christianity.* New Haven: Yale University Press, 2019.

Mussner, Franz. "'Christus (ist) des Gesetzes Ende zur Gerechtigkeit für jeden, der glaubt' (Rom 10,4)." Pages 31–44 in *Paulus—Apostat oder Apostel: Jüdische und christliche Antworten*. Edited by Markus Barth, Josef Blank, Jochanan Bloch, Franz Mussner, and R. J. Zwi Werblowky. Regensburg: Pustet, 1977.

Nanos, Mark. *Reading Paul within Judaism*. Eugene, OR: Cascade Books, 2017.

Nasrallah, Laura. *Archaeology and the Letters of Paul*. Oxford: Oxford University Press, 2019.

Neutel, Karin. "Circumcision Gone Wrong." *Neotestimentica* 50 (2016): 373–96.

———. "Restoring Abraham's Foreskin: The Significance of ἀκροβυστία for Paul's Argument about Circumcision in Romans 4:9–12." *Journal of the Jesus Movement in Its Jewish Setting* 8 (2021): 53–74.

Newman, Amy. "The Death of Judaism in German Protestant Thought from Luther to Hegel." *Journal of the American Academy of Religion* 61 (1993): 455–84.

Nienhuis, David. *Not by Paul Alone: The Formation of the Catholic Epistle Collection and the Christian Canon*. Waco: Baylor University Press, 2007.

Nienhuis, David, and Robert W. Wall. *Reading the Epistles of James, Peter, John and Jude as Scripture: The Shaping and Shape of a Canonical Collection*. Grand Rapids: Eerdmans, 2013.

Novak, David. *The Image of the Non-Jew in Judaism: An Historical and Constructive Study of the Noahide Laws*. Toronto Studies in Theology 14. Lewiston, NY: Mellen, 1983.

Novenson, Matthew V. *Christ among the Messiahs: Christ Language in Paul and Messiah Language in Ancient Judaism*. Oxford: Oxford University Press, 2012.

———. *The Grammar of Messianism: An Ancient Jewish Political Idiom and Its Users*. Oxford: Oxford University Press, 2017.

———. *The Last Man: Judaism and Immortality in the Letters of Paul*. New York: Cambridge University Press, forthcoming.

———, ed. *Monotheism and Christology in Greco-Roman Antiquity*. Supplements to Novum Testamentum 180. Leiden: Brill, 2020.

———. *Paul, Then and Now*. Grand Rapids: Eerdmans, 2022.

Nussbaum, Martha C. *The Therapy of Desire: Theory and Practice in Hellenistic Ethics*. Princeton: Princeton University Press, 1994.

Ophir, Adi, and Ishay Rosen-Zvi. *Goy: Israel's Multiple Others and the Birth of the Gentile*. Oxford: Oxford University Press, 2018.

Origen. *Commentary on the Epistle to the Romans: Books 1–5*. Translated by Thomas P. Scheck. Fathers of the Church 103. Washington, DC: Catholic University of America Press, 2001.

———. *Commentary on the Gospel according to John: Books 13–32*. Translated by Ronald E. Heine. Fathers of the Church 89. Washington, DC: Catholic University of America Press, 1982.

———. *Contra Celsum* [Against Celsus]. Translated by Henry Chadwick. Cambridge: Cambridge University Press, 1965.

——. *Homilies on Genesis and Exodus*. Translated by Ronald E. Heine. Fathers of the Church 71. Washington, DC: Catholic University of America Press, 1993.

——. *On First Principles*. Translated by G. W. Butterworth. New York: Harper & Row, 1966.

Padgett, Alan G. "The Body in Resurrection: Science and Scripture on the 'Spiritual Body' (1 Cor. 15:35–58)." *Word & World* 22 (2002): 155–63.

Parker, Angela. *If God Still Breathes, Why Can't I? Black Lives Matter and Biblical Authority*. Grand Rapids: Eerdmans, 2021.

Pennington, Jonathan. *Heaven and Earth in the Gospel of Matthew*. Grand Rapids: Baker Academic, 2009.

Rowe, C. Kavin. *World Upside Down: Reading Acts in the Graeco-Roman Age*. Oxford: Oxford University Press, 2009.

Russell, Donald A., and David Konstan, ed. and trans. *Heraclitus: Homeric Problems*. Writings from the Greco-Roman World 14. Atlanta: Society of Biblical Literature, 2005.

Sanders, E. P. *Judaism: Practice and Belief (63 BCE–66 CE)*. London: SCM, 1992.

——. *Paul and Palestinian Judaism: A Comparison of Patterns of Religion*. Philadelphia: Fortress, 1977.

Sanfridson, Martin. "Are Circumcision and Foreskin *Really* Nothing? Re-reading 1 Cor. 7:19, Gal. 5:6, and 6:15." *Svensk Exegetisk Årsbok* 86 (2021): 130–47.

Schäfer, Peter. *Judeophobia: Attitudes toward the Jews in the Ancient World*. Cambridge, MA: Harvard University Press, 1997.

Schwartz, Daniel R. "God, Gentiles, and Jewish Law: On Acts 15 and Josephus' Adiabene Narrative." Pages 263–82 in vol. 1 of *Geschichte–Tradition–Reflexion: Festschrift für Martin Hengel zum 70. Geburtstag*. Edited by Peter Schäfer. 3 vols. Tübingen: Mohr Siebeck, 1996.

Schweitzer, Albert. *The Mysticism of Paul the Apostle*. Translated by William Montgomery. Baltimore: Johns Hopkins University Press, 1998.

Scott, Alan. *Origen and the Life of the Stars: A History of an Idea*. Oxford Early Christian Studies. Oxford: Clarendon, 1991.

Simkovich, Malka. *The Making of Jewish Universalism: From Exile to Alexandria*. Lanham, MD: Lexington, 2017.

Smit, Peter-Ben. *Felix Culpa: Ritual Failure and Theological Innovation in Early Christianity*. Supplements to Novum Testamentum 185. Leiden: Brill, 2021.

Smith, James K. A. *The Fall of Interpretation: Philosophical Foundations for a Creational Hermeneutic*. Downers Grove, IL: InterVarsity, 2006.

Smith, Jonathan Z. *Drudgery Divine: On the Comparison of Early Christianities and the Religions of Late Antiquity*. Chicago Studies in the History of Judaism 14. Chicago: University of Chicago Press, 1990.

Smith, Mark S. *The Origins of Biblical Monotheism: Israel's Polytheistic Background and the Ugaritic Texts*. Oxford: Oxford University Press, 2001.

Sommer, Benjamin. *The Bodies of God and the World of Ancient Israel*. Cambridge: Cambridge University Press, 2011.

Stanley, Christopher D. "'Under a Curse': A Fresh Reading of Galatians 3.10–14." *New Testament Studies* 36 (1990): 481–511.

Staples, Jason. *The Idea of Israel in Second Temple Judaism: A New Theory of People, Exile, and Israelite Identity*. Cambridge: Cambridge University Press, 2021.

Stendahl, Krister. "The Apostle Paul and the Introspective Conscience of the West." *Harvard Theological Review* 55 (1962): 119–215.

Stowers, Stanley K. *A Rereading of Romans: Justice, Jews, and Gentiles*. New Haven: Yale University Press, 1994.

——. "What Is 'Pauline Participation in Christ'?" Pages 352–71 in *Redefining First-Century Jewish and Christian Identities: Essays in Honor of Ed Parish Sanders*. Edited by Fabian E. Udoh, Susannah Heschel, Mark Chancey, and Gregory Tatum. Christianity and Judaism in Antiquity 16. Notre Dame: University of Notre Dame Press, 2008.

Tanner, Kathryn. *Christ the Key*. Current Issues in Theology. Cambridge: Cambridge University Press, 2010.

Tappenden, Fred. *Resurrection in Paul: Cognition, Metaphor, and Transformation*. Early Christian Literature 19. Atlanta: SBL Press, 2016.

Tertullian. *Against Praxeas*. Translated by Ernest Evans. London: SPCK, 1948.

Theodoret of Cyrus. *Commentary on the Letters of St. Paul*. Translated by Robert Charles Hill. 2 vols. Brookline, MA: Holy Cross Orthodox Press, 2001.

Thiessen, Matthew. *Contesting Conversion: Genealogy, Circumcision, and Identity in Ancient Judaism and Christianity*. New York: Oxford University Press, 2011.

——. *Jesus and the Forces of Death: The Gospels' Portrayal of Ritual Impurity within First-Century Judaism*. Grand Rapids: Baker Academic, 2020.

——. *Paul and the Gentile Problem*. New York: Oxford University Press, 2016.

——. "'The Rock Was Christ': The Fluidity of Christ's Body in 1 Cor. 10.4." *Journal for the Study of the New Testament* 36 (2013): 103–26.

Trobisch, David. *Paul's Letter Collection*. Minneapolis: Fortress, 1994.

VanderKam, James C., trans. *The Book of Jubilees: A Critical Edition*. Corpus Scriptorum Christianorum Orientalium 511. Leuven: Peeters, 1989.

van Kooten, George. *Cosmic Christology in Paul and the Pauline School: Colossians and Ephesians in the Context of Graeco-Roman Cosmology*. Wissenschaftliche Untersuchungen zum Neuen Testament 2/171. Tübingen: Mohr Siebeck, 2003.

Walsh, Matthew L. *Angels Associated with Israel in the Dead Sea Scrolls: Angelology and Sectarian Identity at Qumran*. Wissenschaftliche Untersuchungen zum Neuen Testament 2/509. Tübingen: Mohr Siebeck, 2019.

Watson, Francis. *Paul and the Hermeneutics of Faith*. London: T&T Clark, 2004.

Weiss, Daniel. "Bloodshed and the Ethics and Theopolitics of the Jewish Dietary Laws." Pages 288–304 in *Feasting and Fasting: The History and Ethics of Jewish Food*. Edited by Aaron S. Gross, Jody Myers, and Jordan D. Rosenblum. New York: New York University Press, 2020.

Wendt, Heidi. *At the Temple Gates: The Religion of Freelance Experts*. Oxford: Oxford University Press, 2016.

Westerholm, Stephen. *Perspectives Old and New on Paul: The "Lutheran" Paul and His Critics*. Grand Rapids: Eerdmans, 2004.

White, Benjamin L. *Remembering Paul: Ancient and Modern Contests over the Image of the Apostle*. Oxford: Oxford University Press, 2014.

Williams, Craig A. *Roman Homosexuality*. 2nd ed. Oxford: Oxford University Press, 2010.

Williams, David. *When the English Fall*. Chapel Hill, NC: Algonquin, 2017.

Wright, N. T. *The Climax of the Covenant: Christ and the Law in Pauline Theology*. Minneapolis: Fortress, 1992.

———. "The Messiah and the People of God: A Study in Pauline Theology with Particular Reference to the Argument of the Epistle to the Romans." PhD diss., University of Oxford, 1991.

———. *Paul and the Faithfulness of God*. Minneapolis: Fortress, 2013.

———. *The Resurrection of the Son of God*. Minneapolis: Fortress, 2002.

Wyschogrod, Michael. *The Body of Faith: God in the People Israel*. Northvale, NJ: Jason Aronson, 1996.

Young, Stephen L. "Ethnic Ethics: Paul's Eschatological Myth of Jewish Sin." *New Testament Studies*, forthcoming.

Zetterholm, Magnus. *Approaches to Paul: A Student's Guide to Recent Scholarship*. Minneapolis: Fortress, 2009.

Author Index

Allison, Dale, 73n5
Aune, David, 86n13

Barclay, John M. G., 8n13, 152
Baron, Lori, 40n6
Barth, Karl, 14
Bauckham, Richard, 76n17
Bazzana, Giovanni B., 124n2
Becker, Adam, 40n6
Berlin, Anne Deborah, 28n6
Boakye, Andrew, 78n20, 131n16
Boccaccini, Gabriele, 150n2
Bos, Abraham P., 107n12
Bowens, Lisa, 21n18
Boyarin, Daniel, 44n12
Brand, Miryam T., 6n9
Bynum, Caroline Walker, 147n24

Campbell, Douglas, 3, 55n10, 69n29, 78n19, 80, 116n6
Campbell, William, 9
Charles, Ronald, 8n14, 44
Chin, C. M., 11
Cohen, Shaye J. D., 85n6
Cohn-Sherbok, Dan, 13n2
Collman, Ryan, 32n14, 90n22

Cook, John Granger, 77n18

Donaldson, Terence L., 18, 45n16, 84n5, 89
Dunn, James D. G., 3, 7, 75, 101, 119n12, 153–54
Duran, Profiat, 28n6

Eco, Umberto, 18
Ehrensperger, Kathy, 9
Ehrman, Bart, 52n4
Eiseland, Nancy, 139n6
Eisenbaum, Pamela, 9, 18, 41, 102n2
Engberg-Pedersen, Troels, 17n7, 107n10, 145
Eyl, Jennifer, 15n4, 53n6

Ferwerda, Rein, 107n12
Fitzgerald, John T., 88n17
Fletcher-Louis, Crispin, 72n3
Fredriksen, Paula, 3, 9, 11, 20, 37, 45n16, 76n17, 85n7, 121

Gaca, Kathy, 65n12
Gaddis, John Lewis, 17

Scripture and Ancient Writings Index